W9-BDV-969

For current pricing information,
or to learn more about this or any Nextext title,
call us toll-free at **1-877-4NX-TEXT**
or visit our website at www.nextext.com.

A CLASSIC RETELLING

Gulliver's Travels

by Jonathan Swift

Printed in the United States of America.

ISBN 0-618-03149-9

1 2 3 4 5 6 7 — QKT — 06 05 04 03 02 01 00

Table of Contents

PART ONE: A VOYAGE TO LILLIPUT

*The reader is introduced to Lemuel Gulliver,
who works for some years as a ship's doctor.
After six years of voyages, he sets out on one
last trip—on a ship bound for the East Indies.
During a fierce storm, the boat overturns.
Gulliver is washed ashore on an island.*

*Gulliver finds that six-inch-tall people have tied
him down while he slept. He meets the Emperor
of the island, which is called Lilliput. He is brought
to the city and, tied by one leg, housed in an
unused temple.*

PART FOUR: A VOYAGE TO THE HOUYHNHNMS

the sailors take over the ship and land Gulliver
on a strange island. There Gulliver meets a
group of tailless monkeylike creatures and a
group of horses who try to communicate
with him.

Gulliver learns a little about the Houyhnhnms
and the Yahoos. He bakes himself a small cake
made of oats.

Gulliver learns the language of the Houyhnhnms.
His master finds out that Gulliver's clothes are
not part of his body.

Gulliver tells his master that horses in England
are made to work for humans like Gulliver
and are never masters.

Gulliver compares and contrasts the Yahoos
to Europeans. Gulliver's descriptions of
wars, dishonesty, and the murderous habits
of Europeans disgust his master.

Gulliver visits the Yahoos and is attacked by a
young female.

*Vocabulary words appear in boldface type and are
footnoted. Specialized or technical words and phrases
appear in lightface type and are footnoted.*

Background

England and Ireland in the Eighteenth Century

Most of the people living in England and Ireland during the eighteenth century were desperately poor. A very small percentage of the population (the nobility and the gentry) controlled the wealth of the two countries. Those who were not a part of the upper class had to struggle to survive.

Hunger and poverty were the main problems in Ireland during the 1700s. Several times over the century, the failure of the potato crop led to widespread hunger. Most families could not afford to send their children to school, so there was little

Engraving A view of London in 1707.

hope that their situation would improve. Because they had had no formal education, most Irish men and women were unable to improve their lives.

In England, things were slightly better, but there was still a great deal of hunger and poverty. To make matters worse, diseases such as smallpox, syphilis, and bubonic plague were killing thousands in London and in surrounding towns and villages. These diseases had no cure, and no medicine helped ease the suffering. The advisors to King George I, the unpopular king who reigned from 1714 to 1727, were unable to help the people of the British Isles. The two major political parties—the Tories and the Whigs—spent far more time fighting each other than they did fighting the hunger and poverty of the people.

Nobility This painting shows the wealth and leisure enjoyed by the upper class in England.

Satire in *Gulliver's Travels*

You can read *Gulliver's Travels* on two levels. First and foremost, it is an adventure story in which the hero, Lemuel Gulliver, travels to four different lands. Each has a strange group of people or animals whose actions often surprise Gulliver.

You can also read *Gulliver's Travels* as a commentary on human nature. Swift used exaggeration, ridicule, irony, and humor to poke fun at eighteenth-century England. This kind of writing is called satire. A summary of the most memorable examples of satire in *Gulliver's Travels* follows.

In Part One, the people of Lilliput are all six inches tall. Because of this, everything they do seems ridiculous. The Emperor (who looks remarkably like Britain's King George I) is a tiny tyrant who believes he has the power and the right to control the world. He insists on all kinds of pomp and ceremony. It would never occur to him that Gulliver could squash him between two fingers.

Swift created another memorable piece of satire in the series of civil wars that broke out. The cause was over the silly question of which end of an egg should be cracked first. This ridiculous disagreement between the Big-Endians and the Small-Endians was Swift's way of criticizing the disagreements between England's political parties.

In Part Two, Gulliver meets the Brobding-nagians, who are as tall as church steeples. These giants are a calm and reasonable group, unlike Gulliver, who is an ordinary man. What Swift was saying here is that ordinary people are not calm and reasonable. They are guided by their emotions and almost always make foolish decisions.

In Part Three, Swift showed what happens when humans are *too* reasonable. Here Swift attacked the universities. Historians, philoso-phers, and scientists are the Laputans, a race of strange people who live on a floating island. Because they are so intelligent, the Laputans can only think on a high level. They have no common sense and are completely unable to perform the simplest everyday tasks. Laputan men spend days

◀ **Laputa** Gulliver's first glimpse of the floating island.

and weeks on mathematical problems or musical scores, even though their houses are falling down and their children are starving.

In Part Four, Swift described the Houyhnhnms, a race of horses that have formed a rational, clean, and honest society. Working for them are the filthy Yahoos, who look and act like humans. The difference between the two groups is meant to highlight the difference between what humans can be and what they usually are. As a result of *Gulliver's Travels,* the word *Yahoo* has come into the English language. It means a "rough, coarse, or uncouth person."

Names and Places

Lemuel Gulliver—the narrator of the *Travels*

Mary Gulliver—Lemuel Gulliver's wife

Johnny and **Betty**—their children

◀ The Lilliputians have tied
Gulliver down.

Part One

Lilliput—an island inhabited by a race of people who are six inches high

Mildendo—the capital of Lilliput

Blefuscu—an island near Lilliput; Lilliput and Blefuscu have been at war
for generations

Golbasto Momaren Evlame Gurdilo Shefin Mull Ully Gue—
The Emperor of Lilliput

Flimnap—Lord High Treasurer of Lilliput; an important advisor to the Emperor

Reldresal—a member of the Lilliputian court and a friend to Gulliver

Mr. John Biddle—captain of the ship that returns Gulliver home from the
land of the tiny people

Part Two

Brobdingnag—a land of giants

Lorbrulgrud—the capital of Brobdingnag

Flanflasnic—one of the King's palaces; located near the seaside

Glumdalclitch—Gulliver's nurse and teacher; she stays with him after he is sold to the Queen

Grildrig—Gulliver's name in the Brobdingnagian language

Mr. Thomas Wilcocks—captain of the ship that rescues Gulliver from his box on the sea and returns him home

▲
Gulliver delights the Brobdingnagians.

Part Three

Laputa—a flying island inhabited by a race of people who can think only in the abstract

Lagado—the capital of the kingdom of Laputa; Lagado is located on Balnibarbi

Balnibarbi—an island that is subject to the rule of the Laputan King

Glubbdubdrib—an island of sorcerers

Luggnagg—a country on the way to Japan from Glubbdubdrib

Struldbrugs—immortal people who live in Luggnagg; they become progressively weaker and more unhappy as they grow older

Part Four

Houyhnhnms—a race of horses that is totally rational and in all ways superior to humans

Yahoos—a race of humanlike creatures that serves the Houyhnhnms

Pedro de Mendez—the ship captain who rescues Gulliver and helps him return to England

▲
Gulliver talks to his Houyhnhnm master.

▲

Jonathan Swift, painted about 1710 when he was in his forties.

Jonathan Swift (1667–1745)

Jonathan Swift was born in Dublin in 1667. His father died before he was born, and his mother moved to England when he was three. He lived with an uncle who, although he had little extra money to spare, managed to send young Jonathan to grammar school and then to college. After college, Swift took a job as secretary to the British political leader

Sir William Temple. During this period, as he learned about politics, he began writing poetry. After an early poem was published, Swift's cousin John Dryden (himself a successful poet) wrote, "Cousin Swift, you will never be a poet."

Swift may have taken Dryden's criticism seriously, because he did not write poetry for a time and began to write essays. His writing style was satiric—he used irony, sarcasm, and ridicule to attack the people, governments, and institutions that he found fault with. After ten years in England, he grew disgusted with politics. In 1713, he accepted a job as dean of St. Patrick's Cathedral in Dublin. While there, he began defending the Irish against the English. Because of his outspokenness, Swift became a hero to the Irish people.

In 1726, Swift published his enormously popular novel *Gulliver's Travels*. Unlike his other works, *Gulliver's Travels* was an immediate success. Readers enjoyed the novel as an exciting travel story as well as a powerful satire of life and politics.

Although Swift received payment for *Gulliver's Travels*, he was unable to make a living by writing. When he was around forty years old, he got a terrible illness. Scholars now believe it might have been Ménière's disease (a disease of the inner ear).

Swift became weaker in the body and in the mind, although he continued to write. It was during this period that he published *A Modest Proposal.* In this brilliant satirical essay, Swift suggests that the problem of overpopulation in Ireland would be solved if the rich Irish people would begin eating the children of the poor for meat.

In his final years, Swift was declared insane. He died in 1745 and was buried in Dublin.

He is now considered to be one of the greatest writers of English prose.

Life of Jonathan Swift

1667—Jonathan Swift is born in Dublin, Ireland. His father dies before he is born. When he is three, his mother moves to England, and Jonathan stays with an uncle in Dublin.

1689—After graduating from Trinity College in Dublin, Swift moves to London and takes a job as a secretary to the Whig statesman and writer, Sir William Temple.

1695—Disillusioned with politics, Swift becomes a minister of the Church of Ireland.

1696—Swift returns to Temple's household, where he stays until Temple dies in 1699.

1704—Swift publishes *Tale of a Tub* in addition to numerous essays and pamphlets.

1710—Swift sides with the Tories, a political party in opposition to the Whigs.

1713—After the Tory government falls, Swift returns to Ireland and becomes dean of St. Patrick's Cathedral in Dublin.

1726—*Gulliver's Travels,* his most successful book, is published.

1729—Swift's essay, *A Modest Proposal* is published.

1742—His body and mind weakened by disease, Swift is declared mentally incompetent.

1745—Swift dies in October. His estate is given to charity.

A CLASSIC RETELLING

Gulliver's *Travels*

A Voyage to Lilliput

My father had a small estate in Nottinghamshire, England. I was the third of five sons. He sent me to Emmanuel College in Cambridge when I was fourteen years old. I stayed at Cambridge three years, until the cost of keeping me in school became too great and I had to leave.

Next I was **apprenticed**[1] to Dr. James Bates, a successful surgeon[2] in London. In four years I learned the skills necessary to become a doctor. At the same time I learned the skills necessary to become a seaman, which I also wanted to be.

When I finished my apprenticeship, the good Dr. Bates referred several patients to me, and I was

---

[1] **apprenticed**—sent to work for a specific amount of time in return for instruction in a trade, an art, or a business.

[2] surgeon—In seventeenth-, eighteenth-, and nineteenth-century England, a physician prescribed medicine, and a surgeon performed most other medical tasks, including surgeries, fixing fractures, treating skin problems and diseases, and so on.

able to set up a **modest**[3] practice. I married Miss Mary Burton, daughter to Mr. Edmund Burton, who gave me four hundred pounds as a **dowry**.[4]

Not long after, my business began to fail, through no fault of my own. After talking with my wife and some of my friends, I decided to go to sea. My plan was to become a ship's doctor, for which there is always a need.

Over the next six years, I made several successful voyages. During my hours of leisure, I read the best authors, ancient and modern, so as to continue my education on my own. When I was ashore, I studied the people and their languages. My good memory was a constant help when it came to understanding the foreign languages.

After so many voyages, however, I grew tired of the sea, and decided to stay at home with my wife and family. For my last trip, I accepted an offer from Captain William Prichard, master of the *Antelope,* who was making a voyage to the South Sea. We set sail from Bristol[5] on May 4, 1699, and our voyage at first was very successful.

Patient reader, I won't trouble you with the details of our trip, except to say that in our passage

---

[3] **modest**—small.

[4] **dowry**—money or property brought by a bride to her husband at marriage.

[5] Bristol—a large city in southwestern England. At one time, Bristol was one of the largest seaports in the world.

to the East Indies,[6] we were struck by a violent storm that threw us well off course. By this time, twelve of our crew were dead from exhaustion or bad food, and the rest were very weak. On November 5, which is the beginning of summer in those parts, the sailors saw a rock that was impossible to avoid. The wind was so strong that we were driven directly upon it, causing the ship to split into two pieces.

Five sailors and I got clear of the ship in a lifeboat. We rowed until we were exhausted and then were forced to leave ourselves to the mercy of the waves. After just a half an hour, however, our small boat was overcome by a sudden storm. What happened to my companions in the boat, I cannot tell, but I believe they were all drowned.

For my own part, I swam as **fortune**[7] directed me, and was pushed forward by wind and tide. When I was half drowned and able to swim no further, I found myself able to touch bottom. I made my way through the surf and landed on shore near eight o'clock in the evening. I walked down the beach for nearly half a mile, but found no sign of houses or people. As I was extremely tired, I lay down to sleep.

---

[6] East Indies—the name East Indies usually refers to Indonesia (the former · Dutch East Indies), but it is sometimes applied to all Southeast Asia and even India.

[7] **fortune**—luck or chance.

After nine hours of sleep, I woke and tried to stand up but was unable to move. I found my arms and legs were strongly fastened on each side to the ground. My hair, which was long and thick, was tied down in the same way. I also felt several thin ropes across my body, from my armpits to my thighs. I heard a confused noise around me but, as I was tied up, I could see nothing except the sky above.

In a short time I felt something alive moving on my left leg. I looked down and saw it was a human creature not six inches high, with a bow and arrow in his hands, and a quiver[1] at his back. In the meantime, I felt at least forty more of the same kind (as I guessed) following the first. I was greatly surprised and yelled so loud that they all

---

[1] quiver—carrying case for arrows.

ran back in a fright. Some of them, as I was after-wards told, were hurt with the falls they got by leaping from my sides to the ground.

However, the little creatures soon returned, and one of them—the first to look upon my face—lifted up his hands and eyes in admiration, and cried out in a shrill but distinct voice, "Hekinah degul!" The others repeated the same words several times, but of course I did not know what they meant. After struggling, I broke the strings that fastened my left arm and the hair on my left side to the ground.

I tried to grab the little creatures, but they ran off a second time before I could seize them. I heard one of them cry aloud, "Tolgo phonac!" At nearly the same time, I felt more than a hundred arrows **discharged**[2] into my left hand, my chest, and my face, all of which pricked me like so many needles. When this shower of arrows was over, I fell back, groaning in grief and pain.

The sting of the arrows hurt very badly. I decided to lie still and wait until night when I would try again to free myself. As for these little people, I was sure that I would be a match for the greatest armies they could bring against me, as they were all so tiny.

---

[2] **discharged**—released.

Such were my plans, but the little people had plans of their own. Over against my right ear, I heard a knocking for more than an hour, like that of people at work. When I turned my head as much as the pegs and strings would let me, I saw a stage had been built about a foot and a half from the ground. Using two ladders, one of the creatures climbed up on the stage and made a long speech, of which I understood not one word. Before he spoke, he called out three times, "Langro dehul san." Just then, about fifty little people cut the strings that fastened the left side of my head. I answered his speech in a few words and held up my hand in a gesture of peace. I showed him how hungry I was by pointing at my mouth.

One of the creatures climbed up on the stage and made a long speech, of which I understood not one word.

The *Hurgo* (for so they call a great lord, as I afterwards learned) understood me very well. He ordered that several ladders should be put up my sides, so that more than a hundred of the little people were able to climb upon my face and walk towards my mouth. They carried with them baskets full of meat and tiny loaves of bread. I was able to eat the contents of two or three baskets in a mouthful and took three loaves of bread in my mouth at a time. They supplied me with as much food as they could and showed all kinds of astonishment at my appetite.

Next I showed them that I wanted to drink. They brought one of their largest barrels of wine, which I drank off in a gulp. They brought me a second barrel, which I drank in the same manner. I made signs for more, but they had none to give me.

After some time, when they saw that I made no more demands for meat, there appeared before me a person of high rank from His Imperial Majesty. This man spoke for about ten minutes, without any signs of anger, but with a determined look on his face. He pointed several times towards a point in the distance—at what I later discovered to be the capital city. He made me understand that His Majesty wished to see me.

I answered in few words, but to no purpose. I must confess that at times I was tempted to grab forty or fifty of these little people and **dash**[3] them upon the ground, but I stopped myself. I remembered the sharpness of their arrows and was sure they were capable of doing me even more harm.

---

[3] **dash**—throw.

Not long after the **dignitary**[4] spoke, I heard the call, "Peplom selan!" Next I felt great numbers of the people on my left side relaxing the cords so that I was able to turn upon my right side. I eased myself by making water,[5] which I very plentifully did, to the great astonishment of these little creatures. They put an ointment on me that took away the pain of the arrows. Fully relieved, I fell into another deep sleep.

While I slept, a machine was built to carry me to the capital city. Five hundred carpenters and engineers prepared the greatest cart they had. It was a frame of wood raised three inches from the ground, about seven feet long and four feet wide. It moved upon twenty-two wheels. I was told later that they pulled me by ropes to where I lay, so that I might be **hoisted**[6] upon the frame. This they did with some effort.

While this whole operation was being accomplished, I lay in a deep sleep, drugged by a potion the little people had slipped into my wine. Fifteen hundred of the Emperor's largest horses, each about

---

[4] **dignitary**—high-ranking person.

[5] making water—urinating.

[6] **hoisted**—raised.

four inches high, were used to pull me towards the **metropolis**,[7] which was half a mile away.

When I awakened again, I found five hundred guards on either side of me. Half of them had torches and half had bows and arrows. All were ready to shoot me if I should move. When we arrived at the gates of the city, the Emperor and all his court came out to meet me. In addition, more than a hundred thousand inhabitants came to see me and wonder. In spite of my guards, more than ten thousand little people climbed upon my body so as to marvel at my size.

> *When I awakened again, I found five hundred guards on either side of me. Half of them had torches and half had bows and arrows. All were ready to shoot me if I should move.*

All the while, a thousand or more workmen **endeavored**[8] to fashion a strong chain, locked with thirty-six padlocks, to my left leg. The other end of the chain they drove into the ground, leaving me two yards of extra rope so that I could move around and even stand up. When I stood up for the first time, the people screamed with astonishment.

---

[7] **metropolis**—major city.

[8] **endeavored**—tried.

The Emperor made it known that an unused temple would be my home. It was about the size of an English dog shed, although it was built much better. When I could stand the sounds and sights of these little people no longer, I crept inside the opening to the temple and lay on its floor. My head was at the rear of the building, and my feet were out the front door. I confess that I had never before felt so sad and alone.

After another deep sleep, I awoke ready to think about my situation. Soon enough, I realized I would have to make the best of things until I could escape. Accordingly, I left the temple and stood up to look around me. Here I must confess that I never saw a more delightful scene. The countryside looked like a garden, and the fields looked like so many beds of flowers. In the woods, the tallest trees were no larger than seven feet tall, although they were perfectly formed. On my left, I was able to see the capital city, which looked like a painted scene of a city in a theater.

For some hours, I had been extremely pressed by the call of nature; which was no wonder, it being almost two days since I had relieved myself. I was, however, caught between feelings of urgency and shame. The best plan I could think of was to creep into my house, which I did. I shut the gate after me, and went as far as the length of my chain would allow. There, in a corner, I discharged my body of that uneasy load. I must say that this was the only time I was ever guilty of so unclean an act. From this time forward, as soon as I rose, I performed that business in open air. Then, every morning due care was taken before company came that the offensive matter should be carried off in wheelbarrows by two servants appointed for that purpose.

His Majesty is taller by almost the breadth of my nail than any of his court, which alone is enough to strike fear into all who see him.

When this adventure was over, I came back out of my house, as I needed fresh air. The Emperor, who had left his tower, came towards me and looked at me with great admiration. He ordered his cooks and butlers to give me food and drink. After twenty carts of meat and ten of drink, I felt able to meet the eyes of the Emperor, who had watched me all the while. His Majesty is taller by almost the breadth of my nail than any of his court, which alone is enough to strike fear into all who see him. His features are strong and masculine. He had an Austrian lip and arched nose, his skin was olive-color, his body and limbs well proportioned, and all his motions graceful. He was then about twenty-eight years old, of which he had reigned for about seven.

His voice was shrill, but very clear, and I could hear it even when I stood up. His clothes were plain and simple. The nobles who stood near him were splendidly dressed. His Imperial Majesty spoke often to me, and I returned answers, but neither of us could understand each other. Several of his priests and lawyers were asked to address themselves to me, and I spoke to them in as many languages as I had the smallest knowledge of— Dutch, Latin, French, Spanish, and Italian—but all to no purpose.

For a **fortnight**[1] or more, large crowds gathered around me almost constantly. During this time, as I discovered later, the Emperor and his Council discussed what should be done with me. They debated what to do if I got loose, how they would talk with me, and how they could afford to feed me. They worried that my diet would be very

---

[1] **fortnight**—two weeks.

expensive and might cause a **famine**.[2] At various times, they came close to voting to starve me, or at least to shoot me in the face and hands with poisoned arrows. But, again and again, they reconsidered, for no other reason than that the smell of so large a **carcass**[3] might produce a **plague**[4] in the city that might very well spread throughout the entire kingdom.

> *At various times, they came close to voting to starve me, or at least to shoot me in the face and hands with poisoned arrows.*

Eventually, the Council and His Majesty came to an agreement that was much in my favor. Each morning, various villages would deliver six cows, forty sheep, and a quantity of bread, wine, and other liquors. Six hundred persons were hired to be my servants. Conveniently, my servants would live in tents on either side of my door. It was also ordered that three hundred tailors would make me a suit of clothes after the fashion of the country. Six of His Majesty's greatest scholars would teach me their language.

---

[2] **famine**—wide-reaching food shortage.

[3] **carcass**—dead body.

[4] **plague**—epidemic disease.

All these orders were followed, and in about three weeks I had made great progress in learning the language of these little people, whom I knew now to be called Lilliputians. During this time, the Emperor often honored me with his visits and was pleased to help my masters teach me. We even began to talk. The first words I learned were the ones I used to beg for liberty, for I was terribly tired of being chained. Each day I would fall to my knees and beg for freedom. His answer, as I could understand it, was that first I must *lumos kelmin pesso desmar lon Emposo;* that is, swear a peace with him and his kingdom. In the meantime, I would be treated with kindness and allowed to prove my loyalty.

First, said the Emperor, I must hand over my sword, **scabbard**[5] and all. Very slowly, to show that I meant no harm, I drew my sword, which was quite bright, although a little rusted from the sea water. When I did so, all the troops gave a shout of terror and surprise, for the reflection of the sun on the sword dazzled their eyes. His Majesty, who was quite brave, ordered me to return it to the scabbard,

---

[5] **scabbard**—covering for a dagger or sword.

and I put it on the ground as gently as I could, about six feet from the end of my chain.

The next thing he demanded I hand over was what he called the hollow iron pillars, which I knew to be my pistols. After I drew them out, the Emperor asked to see how they worked. I warned him not to be afraid, and then loaded one of the pistols with gunpowder. After another warning, I shot it into the air. The astonishment here was much greater than at the sight of my sword. Hundreds fell down as if they had been struck dead. Even the Emperor, although he stood his ground, could not recover himself for a moment or two. I handed over both my pistols and then my pouch of powder and bullets. Then I gave up my silver and copper money, my purse with nine large pieces of gold, my knife and razor, my comb and silver snuffbox,[6] my handkerchief, and my journal-book. In a secret pocket on my vest that they did not find, I kept my **spectacles**[7] and several other little things. Being of no importance to the Emperor, I did not think them necessary to turn over.

Hundreds fell down as if they had been struck dead.

---

[6] snuffbox—a very small box for holding snuff, a powdered tobacco that was popular during Swift's time.

[7] **spectacles**—glasses.

M y good behavior so impressed the Emperor and his court that I began to believe that I would have my freedom in just a short time. I did everything I could to show them that I meant no harm. Gradually, the Lilliputians grew used to me. I would sometimes lie down and let five or six of them dance on my hand. At last, the boys and girls would come and play hide-and-seek in my hair. All the while, I made good progress in understanding and speaking their language.

About two or three days before I was set free from my chains, His Majesty received a message that some of his subjects who had been riding near the place where I was first captured had seen a great black object lying on the ground. It was no living creature, they said, but it was very large and hollow inside. They humbly guessed that it might belong to the Man-Mountain, which is what they called me. If His Majesty would permit it, his subjects would bring the object to the capital city. I knew what they meant and was glad that they had found my hat. I begged His Majesty to have it brought to me, which he graciously agreed to do. Not long after, my hat arrived and I put it on my head, to the delight of all who stood and watched.

Two days after this adventure, the Emperor had an idea that struck him as brilliant. He desired me to stand like a Colossus,[1] with my legs as far apart as I could manage. He then ordered his General to draw up his troops in close order, and march them under me, with drums beating, colors flying, and **pikes**[2] advanced. His Majesty ordered that, upon pain of death, every soldier in the march should avoid embarrassing me. But, to confess the truth, my pants were at that time in so poor a condition that some turned up their eyes as they passed under me and laughed.

After I had many, many times asked for my liberty, His Majesty and his Council agreed to give me more freedom. First, however, I would have to agree to a set of conditions, which I record here in translation:

---

[1] Colossus—referring to the Colossus of Rhodes, a huge statue of Helios, the Greek god of the sun. It is one of the seven wonders of the ancient world.

[2] **pikes**—long spears.

Conditions Set Forth by
The Emperor Golbasto Momaren Evlame Gurdilo
Shefin Mull Ully Gue and Council

The Man-Mountain shall not depart from our lands without our permission.

He shall not come into our city unless our people have been given two hours' warning to keep within their doors.

The Man-Mountain shall only walk on our major roads and not lie down in any of our meadows or fields.

As he walks on the said roads, he shall take care not to step on any of our loving subjects, their horses, or carriages, nor pick up any of our subjects without their consent.

If an urgent message has to be carried, the Man-Mountain will carry the messenger and horse in his pocket and return them safely.

He shall be our ally against our enemies on the Island of Blefuscu and do his best to destroy their fleet, which is now preparing to invade us.

The Man-Mountain shall, in two months' time, deliver an exact measurement of the distance around our lands. This he will accomplish by counting the number of steps it takes him to travel around the island.

Lastly, upon his solemn oath to observe all the above articles, the Man-Mountain shall have a daily allowance of meat and drink sufficient for the support of 1,728 of our subjects, with free access to the Emperor.

I agreed to these articles with great cheerfulness, although some of them were not so honorable as I could have wished. Afterwards, my chains were unlocked, and I was at full liberty. The Emperor did me the honor of observing the whole ceremony. I showed my gratitude by **prostrating**[3] myself at his feet; but he commanded me to rise and said he hoped I should prove to be a useful servant.

---

[3] **prostrating**—lying face downward on the ground.

The first request I made after I was freed was that I might be allowed to see Mildendo, the capital city. The Emperor agreed to my request, on condition that I would not hurt the people or their houses, and said that I might come later that day.

The wall surrounding Mildendo is two-and-a-half feet high. I stepped over the great gate and walked very gently down the two main streets. I wore my short **waistcoat**,[1] for I was afraid of damaging the roofs and eaves of the houses with the edges of my coat. The attic windows and tops of houses were so crowded with spectators that I thought in all my travels I had not seen a more **populous**[2] place.

---

[1] **waistcoat**—vest.

[2] **populous**—heavily populated.

The city is an exact square, each side of the wall being five hundred feet long. The two great streets, which divide it into four quarters, are five feet wide. The lanes and alleys, which I could not enter, are from twelve to eighteen inches wide. The town is capable of holding five hundred thousand souls. Each house is from three to five stories tall, and the shops and markets are well stocked and attractive.

The Emperor's palace is in the center of the city where the two great streets meet. His Majesty wished me to see the magnificence of his palace; but this I was not able to do till three days later. I finally **contrived**[3] to lie down upon my side and press my face up to the windows. Inside I discovered the most splendid rooms that can be imagined. I also saw the **Empress**[4] and the young Princes, with their servants about them. Her Imperial Majesty was pleased to smile very graciously upon me and gave me—out of the window—her hand to kiss.

I discovered the most splendid rooms that can be imagined.

---

[3] **contrived**—worked out a way.
[4] **Empress**—wife of the Emperor.

One morning, about two weeks later, an official named Reldresal, who is the Emperor's Secretary of Private Affairs, came to my house to speak with me. I offered to lie down, so that he might more easily reach my ear; but he chose rather to let me hold him in my hand during our conversation.

He began by explaining how difficult things had become in court. The Lilliputians, he said, were in danger of an invasion from the island of Blefuscu, which is the other great empire of the universe and almost as large and powerful as that of Lilliput. Blefuscu is, in fact, ruled by His Majesty's brother.

"For years and years," Reldresal explained, "the Lilliputians and Blefuscudians have been engaged in a most **obstinate**[5] war." He then went on to tell me that the war started over an issue of some importance to His Majesty: on which end an egg shall be broken before it is eaten. His Majesty breaks an egg on the smaller end and insists that his subjects do so as well. The Blefuscudians—and some Lilliputians—say they must be given the right to start with the larger end of the egg, if they so choose.

---

[5] **obstinate**—stubborn.

"Over the years," Reldresal continued, "there have been no less than six rebellions in Lilliput. Each time the Blefuscudians lent their support to the revolutionary Big-Endian Lilliputians. All told, close to eleven thousand persons have suffered death rather than break their eggs at the smaller end."

"Close to eleven thousand persons have suffered death rather than break their eggs at the smaller end."

Then Reldresal told me the worst news of all. He explained that the Blefuscudians had created a tremendous fleet of large, powerful ships and were planning to invade Lilliput. His Imperial Majesty, having great confidence in my courage and strength, therefore commanded me to help save Lilliput.

I told Reldresal to let the Emperor know that, although I felt it would not be right for me, a foreigner, to interfere in this war, I would be ready to risk my life to defend His Highness and Lilliput against all invaders.

The Empire of Blefuscu is an island situated to the north-northeast side of Lilliput. Lilliput and Blefuscu are divided by a channel that is eight hundred yards wide. Since all communication between Blefuscu and Lilliput was strictly forbidden, the Blefuscudians had not heard of me. After speaking with Reldresal, I avoided appearing on that side of the coast, for fear of being seen by some of the enemy's ships.

After a little thought, I communicated to His Majesty that I had a plan to seize the enemy's entire fleet, which lay at anchor in the harbor ready to sail. I consulted the most experienced Lilliputian seamen about the depth of the channel. They told me that in the middle it was seventy glumgluffs deep, which is about six feet, and that the rest of the channel was fifty glumgluffs at most.

After taking a secret look at the enemy's fleet, I thought up a plan. I asked for a large quantity of the strongest cable and bars of iron that the Lilliputians could find. I **trebled**[1] the cable to make it stronger. Then I twisted three of the iron bars together, with a hook at the end. After I had fixed fifty hooks to as many cables, I went to the northeast coast, took off my coat, shoes, and stockings, and walked into the channel. I waded as long as I could and swam in the middle about thirty yards till I felt ground; I arrived at the enemy fleet in less than half an hour.

The enemy sailors were so frightened when they saw me that they leaped out of their ships.

The enemy sailors were so frightened when they saw me that they leaped out of their ships and swam to their shore. There I saw another thirty thousand astonished, terrified people. With all of Blefuscu watching, I took my hooks and cable and fastened one ship to another. As I worked, the enemy shot several thousand arrows, many of which stuck in my hands and face and disturbed me. (To protect my eyes, I pulled out my spectacles, which still lay hidden in my vest pocket.) When I was finished,

---

[1] **trebled**—twisted three parts together to make one.

I took up the knotted end of the cables to which my hooks were tied and easily drew fifty of the enemy's man-of-war[2] ships after me. The Blefuscudians, who had not the least idea of what I was planning, were astonished. When they saw that I was taking their entire fleet, they sent up a scream of grief and despair that is impossible to describe. Once I had moved out of danger, I stopped a while to pick out the arrows that stuck in my hands and face and took off my spectacles. Then I began wading across the channel. Not long after, I arrived safely at the royal port of Lilliput, dragging with me the Blefuscudian fleet.

I arrived safely at the royal port of Lilliput, dragging with me the Blefuscudian fleet.

The Emperor and his whole court stood on the shore awaiting my arrival. When I was close enough to be heard, I cried out, "Long live the Emperor of Lilliput!"

Well pleased with my actions, the great prince named me Nardac, the highest title among the Lilliputians. His Majesty immediately asked me to bring the rest of the enemy's ships across the channel. He seemed to think nothing of destroying

---

[2] man-of-war—a combat ship.

the entire fleet. He clearly loved the idea of reducing Blefuscu into a part of his own country, of destroying the Big-Endian exiles, and of forcing the people to break the smaller end of their eggs. He would be the only ruler of both territories.

I convinced his Council that this would be wrong, that to enslave an entire nation would be a matter of cruelty, and that I would have no part of it. His Majesty never forgave this open rebellion on my part. From this moment forward, there was a tension between myself and some members of his court. Still, my thievery of the enemy's fleet had the desired effect. About three weeks after this adventure, a solemn embassy arrived from Blefuscu with humble offers of a peace, which His Majesty most graciously accepted.

Some time after my adventures with the Blefuscu fleet, I was awakened at midnight with the cries of many hundred people at my door. I heard the word *burglum* repeated over and over. When I appeared, several of the Emperor's court were making their way through the crowd. They begged me to come immediately to the palace, as Her Imperial Majesty's apartment was on fire. I got dressed in an instant and hurried to the palace.

Upon arriving, I saw that the palace fire had grown so large that their many thimble-sized buckets of water were of no use. I might easily have snuffed it out with my coat, but I had left that behind in my haste to be of help.

It was clear to me that the palace might burn to the ground unless I could find a way to help. Fortunately, that night, before I had retired, I had drunk a large quantity of good Lilliputian wine. By the luckiest chance in the world, I had not discharged any of it. Without delay, I began to void my urine in such quantity, and applied it so well to the proper places, that in three minutes the fire was out, and the palace was saved from destruction.

In the morning, I waited for the Emperor's thanks and congratulations, although I was concerned because of the way I had performed the rescue. The Emperor did thank me graciously, although he and his Council felt some disgust with what I had done. Later, I was told that the Empress, having the greatest **abhorrence**[3] for my deed, had promised never to use that part of the palace again and vowed revenge.

---

[3] **abhorrence**—disgust, hatred.

I stayed on the fair island of Lilliput for nine months and thirteen days and learned much about the laws and customs of Lilliput. During this time, I made enough furniture to make my home as comfortable as might be reasonably expected. Two hundred seamstresses were hired full time to make what **linens**[1] and clothes I required. I had three hundred cooks to prepare my food, and a hundred or more served me while I ate. I found the meat and wine to be excellent. At times, His Majesty and members of his court joined me for dinner.

One evening, Flimnap, the Lord High Treasurer, came with His Majesty. Flimnap had always been my secret enemy, though he outwardly showed all kinds of respect and admiration. This particular

---

[1] **linens**—shirts and sheets.

evening, Flimnap was in a terrible mood, as he had spent the day counting the funds in his treasury. He was very much **dismayed**[2] that the amount of money in the treasury had recently become very much smaller. After considering the amount of money it took to clothe and feed me, he told His Majesty in no uncertain terms that I should be sent away.

To make matters far worse, Flimnap had become jealous of me because of his wife. There had been some gossip in town that this excellent woman had some affection for me. This I solemnly declare to be a terrible lie. I admit that Her Grace came often to my house, but only as a gesture of kindness and friendship, and never without her sister and daughter and a whole group of servants. On those occasions, when a servant announced that I had visitors, I would go immediately to the door; and, after paying my respects, take up the coach and two horses very carefully in my hands and place them on a table. There I had built a moveable rim of five inches high to prevent accidents. Then I would sit down, leaning my face toward my company, and engage in the most pleasant of conversations. While I was busy with my

---

[2] **dismayed**—alarmed.

visitors, the coachmen would gently drive the others round my table. I passed many an afternoon very happily this way.

I challenge the Treasurer, or anyone else of the court, to prove that any of these visitors ever came secretly, for not a soul ever did except the secretary Reldresal. And yet these rumors caused me to lose all credit with Flimnap and gradually with the Emperor himself, as Flimnap was one of his most trusted advisors.

Before I tell of my leaving this kingdom, it may be proper to inform the reader of a plot that had been forming against me for two months. My enemies in the court, led by Flimnap, had accused me of treason against His Majesty and the state. This charge was, of course, untrue but, as I have said, I was not without enemies, and they were determined to see me **exiled**.[3] They accused me of working with the Blefuscudian government to overthrow the King of Lilliput. This was a lie, as I had nothing but a deep and **abiding**[4] respect for His Royal Highness, the Emperor of Lilliput.

---

[3] **exiled**—forced out of the country; banished.

[4] **abiding**—long-lasting.

Still, the Council was able to convince the Emperor that the charge of **treason**[5] was true. Regarding the issue of exile, His Majesty was inclined to show much mercy towards me. He spoke of my great services to the Crown and to the island of Lilliput in general. Flimnap disagreed, saying that I had caused more problems than I had solved, and that I should be put to death in a most painful manner. This, he said, was the only punishment appropriate for the crime of treason.

The Council ordered that my eyes be put out by arrow or poison, and that the deed be done as quickly as possible.

Fortunately for me, His Majesty and my other supporters won the debate. My life would be spared, they decided, although my punishment would be to lose my sight. The Council ordered that my eyes be put out by arrow or poison, and that the deed be done as quickly as possible. Those who had hoped for me to be put to death were unhappy with the Council's decision. They vowed to slowly starve me to death, although they planned to do this in secret, so as not to openly go against the court.

---

[5] **treason**—betrayal of your country or ruler.

I determined that I would save myself—
and my eyes—at all cost. Not wanting to harm
the island on which I had found happiness and
temporary safety, I decided that I would have to
leave at once. I took the opportunity to send a letter
to the Emperor of Blefuscu, telling him that I
would visit him.

Without waiting for an answer, I went to the
side of the island where the Lilliput fleet lay. I
grabbed a large man-of-war, tied a cable to the
bow, and began wading and swimming, with the
boat in tow. I arrived safely at the royal port of
Blefuscu and was guided to the capital city, where
the Emperor awaited my arrival. Upon catching
sight of the royal party, I lay upon the ground to
kiss His Majesty's and the Empress's hand. I told
His Majesty that I had come with permission,
without mentioning a word of my disgrace.

Three days after my arrival on Blefuscu, I saw, about half a league[1] off, in the sea, something that looked like an overturned boat—a boat made by men of my size. I pulled off my shoes and stockings and waded until I came within a hundred yards of the boat, after which I was forced to swim. To my surprise, I found the object to be a real boat, which I assumed was washed up by a recent storm.

With the help of three thousand seamen from the Blefuscudian navy, I was able to fasten a cable to the boat and pull it to shore. Then, with the help of two thousand men with ropes and engines, I was able to turn it over on its bottom and found it was only a little damaged.

I shall not trouble the reader with the difficulties of making small repairs, carving oars, and

---

[1] league—about three miles.

generally making the boat seaworthy again. I told the Emperor of Blefuscu that good fortune had thrown the boat in my way and that it was meant to carry me somewhere from which I could return to my own country. I asked His Majesty's help in getting materials to fit it up,[2] together with his permission to leave, which he was pleased to grant.

While I was working on the boat, the Emperor of Lilliput sent a messenger to Blefuscu with the message that I was to return to Lilliput immediately. This **envoy**[3] had instructions to explain to the monarch of Blefuscu the charges against me and also to inform the court of the great **leniency**[4] of my sentence. To lose one's eyes, the envoy was ordered to tell us, was a very small price to pay for the crime of treason. The envoy also informed us that His Imperial Majesty viewed my departure from Lilliput as an act of treason, and if I did not return within two hours, I would lose my title of Nardac and be declared a traitor. The envoy added that in order to maintain the peace between both empires, his master expected that His Royal Highness of Blefuscu would give orders to have

---

[2] **fit it up**—get it ready to sail.

[3] **envoy**—government representative on a special diplomatic mission.

[4] **leniency**—mercifulness; state of not being severe. This, of course, is a joke.

me sent to Lilliput, bound hand and foot, to be punished as a traitor.

The Emperor of Blefuscu, after taking three days to consult, returned an answer consisting of many **civilities**[5] and excuses. He said that as for sending me back, it was impossible. Although I had stolen Blefuscu's fleet, I had begun to make myself useful to the Blefuscudians, and I was welcome to stay as long as it took to prepare my vessel and make my way back out to sea.

Then the monarch of Blefuscu told me that if I would continue in his service, he would offer his gracious protection. Although I believed he was sincere, I had decided to put no more confidence in princes or ministers. Therefore, with thanks for his favorable intentions, I humbly asked to be allowed to leave. I told him that since fortune, whether good or evil, had thrown a boat in my way, I was resolved to risk a voyage in the ocean, rather than be an occasion of difference between two such mighty monarchs.

The disagreement between Lilliput and Blefuscu caused me to move up my departure date.

---

[5] **civilities**—polite words.

The Blefuscudian Court, impatient to have me gone because I was such a drain on their budget, readily gave me all that I needed. Five hundred workmen made two sails for my boat. I took the time to make ropes and cables by twisting together ten, twenty, or thirty of the strongest and thickest of theirs. A great stone that I found would serve as my anchor.

In about a month, when all was ready, I prepared to take my leave. When the Emperor and royal family came out of the palace, I lay down on my face to kiss His Grace's hand, which he very graciously gave me. His Majesty presented me with fifty purses of two hundred gold pieces apiece, together with his picture at full length, which I put immediately into one of my gloves to keep it from being hurt.

I had loaded the boat with the bodies of a hundred oxen and three hundred sheep, in addition to bread, drink, and as much salted meat as four hundred cooks could provide. I took with me six cows and two bulls alive, and the same number of **ewes** and **rams**,[6] intending to carry them into my own country and **propagate**[7] the breed. To feed them, I had a good bundle of hay and a bag of corn.

---

[6] **ewes** and **rams**—female and male sheep.

[7] **propagate**—reproduce by breeding.

I would gladly have taken a dozen of the natives, but the Emperor would by no means permit this.

Having thus prepared all things as well as I was able, I set sail on September 24, 1701, at six in the morning. When I had gone about four leagues[8] northward, I arrived at a small island. I cast anchor on the lee side[9] of the island, which seemed to be uninhabited. I then took some refreshment and went to sleep immediately.

The next morning, I ate my breakfast before the sun was up. Heaving anchor, I steered the same course that I had done the day before, directed by my pocket compass. My intention was to reach, if possible, an inhabited island. I discovered nothing all that day. Upon the next day, about three in the afternoon, I spied a large sail steering to the southeast. I called her, but could get no answer; yet I found I gained upon her, for the wind slackened. It is not easy to express the joy I felt at the hope of once more seeing my beloved country and the dear family I had left behind. The large ship

> *I would gladly have taken a dozen of the natives, but the Emperor would by no means permit this.*

[8] four leagues—about twelve miles, with each league equaling about three miles.

[9] lee side—side sheltered from the wind.

loosened her sails, and I came up with her between five and six in the evening of September 26. My heart was full of happiness at the sight of English colors on her flag. I put the cows and sheep into my coat pockets and got on board with all my little cargo of food.

The vessel was an English merchant ship, returning from Japan by the North and South Seas. The captain, a Mr. John Biddle of Deptford, was a very polite man and an excellent sailor. The captain treated me with kindness and asked me to tell him from what place I had come last. I explained what I could, but he thought I was **raving**[10] and that the dangers I had undergone in my small boat had disturbed my head. Then I took my black cattle and sheep out of my pocket. These clearly convinced him of the truth of what I said. I then showed him the gold given to me by the Emperor of Blefuscu, together with His Majesty's picture at full length, and some other rarities of that country. I gave him two purses of two hundred sprugs each. I also promised, when we arrived in England, to make him a present of a cow and a sheep big with young.

---

[10] **raving**—talking like someone who is crazy.

I shall not trouble the reader with a particular account of this voyage, which went well for the most part. We arrived in England on April 13, 1702. I had only one misfortune. The rats on board carried away one of my sheep. I found her bones in a hole, picked clean from the flesh. I got the rest of my cattle safe on shore and set them grazing on a bowling green[11] at Greenwich, where the fineness of the grass made them feed very heartily. The short time I continued in England, I made great profit by showing my cattle to many audiences. Before I began my second voyage, I sold them for six hundred pounds.

I stayed only two months with my wife and family, for my **insatiable**[12] desire of seeing foreign countries would allow me to stay no longer. I left fifteen hundred pounds with my wife and set her up in a good house at Redriff. My son, Johnny, was at the grammar school[13] and was an intelligent, happy child. My daughter Betty (who is now well married, and has children) was then at her needle-work. I took leave of my wife and boy and girl, with tears on both sides, and went on board the

[11] bowling green—smooth lawn used for games such as bowls.
[12] **insatiable**—impossible to satisfy.
[13] grammar school—secondary school.

Adventure, a merchant ship of three hundred tons, bound for Surat, a country in India. Captain John Nicholas of Liverpool was the commander. But my account of this voyage must be referred to the second part of my travels.

THE END OF THE FIRST PART

A Voyage to
Brobdingnag

H aving been condemned by nature and for-tune to an active and restless life, two months after my return from Lilliput, I again left my native country. Under the capable direction of Captain John Nicholas and his sturdy boat, we made excel-lent progress. We arrived soon at the Cape of Good Hope,[1] where we landed for fresh water. Upon our arrival, we discovered a leak in the boat, so we unloaded our goods and stayed at the Cape for the winter.

At the end of March, we set sail again and had a good voyage until we passed through the straits of Madagascar.[2] On April 19, however, the wind began to blow with much more force, and we

---

[1] Cape of Good Hope—a small, rocky peninsula that juts into the Atlantic Ocean near the southern tip of Africa.

[2] Madagascar—an island nation in the Indian Ocean, located about 250 miles from the southeastern coast of Africa.

were blown off course. On May 2, the captain told us to prepare for a storm, which he sensed was on its way. The next day, a southern wind, called a **monsoon**,[3] began to howl.

For a long time, the ship rode out the storm quite bravely. We did our best to man the sails and waited nervously for the wind to die down. After many anxious days we found that we had been blown into a part of the world that even the oldest sailor on our ship could not recognize. Still, our food held out well, and our crew was all in good health. We were in some need of fresh water, but we thought it best to continue on rather than try and make our way back to known territory.

> *We had been blown into a part of the world that even the oldest sailor on our ship could not recognize.*

On June 16, 1703, a boy on the topmast[4] saw land. On the 17th, we came in full view of a great island or continent (for we knew not which). We cast anchor within a league of the island, and our captain sent a dozen well-armed men (myself included) in the longboat,[5] with vessels for water if

---

[3] **monsoon**—wind from the southwest or south that brings heavy rainfall.

[4] topmast—tall pole that rises from the deck of a sailing vessel to support the sails.

[5] longboat—the largest boat carried by a sailing ship.

any could be found. When we came to land, we saw no river or spring, nor any sign of people. Our men therefore wandered on the shore to find some fresh water, and I walked alone about a mile on the other side, where I noticed that the country was bare and rocky. I now began to tire, and seeing nothing to interest me, I returned down towards the creek. As I approached the sea, I was startled to see our men already in the longboat, rowing quickly towards the ship. I yelled after them although they were too far away to hear me.

All of a sudden, I observed a huge creature walking after them in the sea as fast as he could. He waded not much deeper than his knees and took **prodigious**[6] strides, but our men had the lead, and the monster was not able to overtake the boat. I dared not wait to see the outcome, but I ran as fast as I could and climbed a steep hill. To my surprise, I saw huge fields of freshly cut grass. What surprised me was the length of the grass, which was about twenty feet high.

After a little searching, I found a footpath, which I followed for quite some time. Soon, I saw

---

[6] **prodigious**—enormous.

another creature, this one quite as large as the one who had chased the boat. I was struck with fear and astonishment, and ran to hide myself in the grass. I heard him calling out in a voice louder than a clap of thunder. After his call, several monsters like himself came out from the fields, each with reaping hooks[7] and scythes[8] in their hands. These people were not so well dressed as the first, so I assumed that they were servants or laborers of some type.

> *I lay down between two ridges and heartily wished I might there end my days.*

Being quite exhausted and wholly overcome by grief and despair, I lay down between two ridges and heartily wished I might there end my days. I bemoaned[9] the fate of my poor wife and children. I mourned my own stupidity in attempting a second voyage against the advice of all my friends and relations.

Although I was badly frightened, I knew there was no point in giving myself over to negative thoughts. The giants were fast approaching, and I was afraid that I would be squashed underfoot at

---

[7] reaping hooks—tools used to cut grain for harvest.

[8] scythes—tools with long, curved blades that are used for mowing or reaping.

[9] **bemoaned**—grieved about.

any moment. With nothing left to do, I opened my mouth and screamed as loud as I could. The creature who was closest to me stopped and looked round. At last he saw me and took hold of me like one would lay hold of a small animal that was likely to bite or scratch. After another moment, he brought me within three yards of his eyes so that he could see my shape more perfectly. I tried not to struggle, although he held me about sixty feet from the ground and was pinching me quite painfully. I raised my eyes toward the sun and clasped my hands together as if I were praying. I wanted to give him the idea that I meant him no harm, although of course he had no reason to be afraid of a creature as small as I. He seemed to understand my meaning, however. He placed me as gently as possible into his coat pocket and ran along to his master, who was the same person I had first seen in the field.

The master looked at me in astonishment and called several workers around him. He asked (I afterwards learned) whether they had ever seen in the fields any little creature that resembled me. He placed me softly on the ground upon all fours, but I got immediately up, and walked slowly backwards and forwards, to let those people see I had no intention of running away. They all sat down in a circle about me, the better to observe my motions. I pulled off my hat, and made a low bow towards the farmer. I fell on my knees, and lifted up my hands and eyes, and spoke several words as loud as I could.

Next I took a purse of gold out of my pocket and humbly presented it to the farmer. He took it on the palm of his hand and then looked closely at it, but he could make nothing of it. Then I made a sign that he should place his hand on the ground. I took the purse and, opening it, poured all the gold into his palm. I saw him wet the tip of his little finger upon his tongue and take up one of my largest pieces, and then another, but he did not understand what they were. He made me a sign to put them again into my purse, and the purse again into my pocket, which after offering it to him several times, I thought it best to do.

The farmer by this time was convinced I must be a rational creature. He spoke often to me, but the sound of his voice pierced my ears like that of a thunderstorm. I answered as loud as I could, in several languages, and he often laid his ear within two yards of me, but it was no use, because we couldn't understand each other. He then sent his servants to their work and, taking his handkerchief out of his pocket, spread it on his left hand and made me a sign to step into it. I could easily do this, for it was not above a foot in thickness. I thought it best to do as he wished and, for fear of falling, laid myself at length upon the handkerchief, which he then tied into a gentle knot. In this manner, he carried me to his house.

As soon as we arrived, he called out to his wife and showed me to her; but she screamed and ran back, as women in England do at the sight of a toad or a spider. However, when she had seen my behavior and how well I observed the signs her husband made, she was **reconciled**[10] and soon became extremely fond of me.

As it was about noon, a servant brought in dinner. The meal consisted of one substantial dish of meat that was in a pot of perhaps twenty-four feet in diameter. The company were the farmer and his wife, three children, and an old grandmother. When they sat down, the farmer placed me at some distance from him on the table, which was thirty feet high from the floor. I was terribly frightened and

---

[10] **reconciled**—won over to friendliness.

kept as far as I could from the edge for fear of falling. The wife chopped a bit of meat then crumbled some bread on a saucer and placed it before me. I made her a low bow, took out my knife and fork, and fell to eating, which amused them. The wife sent her maid for a small cup, which held about three gallons, and filled it with drink. I took up the vessel with much difficulty in both hands and, in a most respectful manner, drank to her ladyship's health. My words, spoken as loud as I could in English, made the company laugh so heartily that I was almost deafened with the noise. This drink tasted like a **cider**[11] and was not unpleasant.

Next my master (as I shall henceforth call him) made signs that he wanted me to approach. Before I could make my way across the table, however, his youngest son, a boy about ten years old grabbed me and held me high in the air, which made me shake with fear. Luckily, his father snatched me back again, and at the same time gave the boy a **box**[12] on the ear that would have felled a troop of horses. But being afraid the boy might

> *A boy about ten years old grabbed me and held me high in the air, which made me shake with fear.*

---

[11] **cider**—juice pressed from fruit.

[12] **box**—slap or blow.

hold a grudge against me and well remembering how mischievous all children can be with sparrows, rabbits, young kittens, and puppy dogs, I fell on my knees. Pointing to the boy, I made my master understand that I desired his son might be pardoned.

In the middle of dinner, my mistress's favorite cat leaped into her lap. I heard a noise behind me like that of a dozen stocking weavers at work. Turning my head, I found it came from the purring of this animal, who seemed to be three times larger than an ox. I must admit that this cat terrified me, although my mistress did not allow the cat to get near me. How strange, I thought, to have all these new enemies: boys and cats and who knew what else.

How strange, I thought, to have all these new enemies: boys and cats and who knew what else.

When dinner was almost done, the nurse came in with a child a year old in her arms, who immediately spied me and began a squall[13] that you might have heard all around the world. Clearly, she wanted me for a plaything. Unfortunately, the mother took me up and held me out to the child, who quickly seized

---

[13] squall—cry or scream.

me by the middle and got my head in her mouth. I roared so loud that the child was frightened and let me drop. I would have broken my neck if the mother had not held her apron under me.

When dinner was done, my master went out to his laborers, after telling his wife to take care of me. I was tired and longed to sleep, so my mistress put me on her own bed and covered me with a clean, white handkerchief that was larger than the sail of a man-of-war. I slept about two hours and dreamed I was at home with my wife and children. So I felt even worse when I awakened to find myself in a large room lying on a bed that was at least twenty yards wide and fifteen yards tall.

M y mistress had a daughter of nine years old, who was quite advanced in her needlework. She and her mother fitted up a cradle for me, along with a fresh set of clothes. She made me seven shirts and some other linen, and these she constantly washed for me with her own hands. She was also my teacher. When I pointed to anything, she told me the name of it in her own tongue, so that in a few days I was able to call for whatever I needed. She was very good-natured and not more than forty feet high, being little for her age. She gave me the name of Grildrig, which the family took up, and afterwards the whole kingdom. I called her my Glumdalclitch, or little nurse.

It now began to be known in the neighborhood that my master had found a strange creature in the field, about the size of a *splacknuck*, but exactly shaped in every part like a human creature. It seemed to speak a little language of its own, went on two legs, and was tame and gentle. A farmer who lived nearby came to find out if the story was true, and my master immediately produced me, to the man's amazement. This man then had the idea to show me as a sight at the market the next day, which was as miserable an idea as I've ever heard, but of course I had no say in the matter.

The next morning, my master put me in a box and carried me to market in a neighboring town. He brought along his little daughter, who wanted to keep an eye upon

My master, to avoid a crowd, would allow only thirty people at a time to see me.

me and protect me from harm. Upon arrival at the market, I was placed on a table in the largest room of the inn. My master, to avoid a crowd, would allow only thirty people at a time to see me. Not surprisingly, I was quite an attraction, which greatly pleased him. Realizing how profitable I might be, he began to make plans to travel with me throughout the kingdom, which, I learned, was called Brobdingnag.

With his wife's consent, we set out on our journey on August 17, 1703. My master brought Glumdalclitch with us, which was fortunate for me as she was my best protector. My master's plan was to show me in small towns and large cities alike. We made excellent progress and arrived in the capital city, called Lorbrulgrud, or Pride of the Universe, sometime in September. My master rented a huge room in Lorbrulgrud and planned to show me to as many people as he could. I was shown ten times a day to the wonder and satisfaction of all people. I could now speak the language reasonably well and perfectly understood every word that was spoken to me.

However, all of this caused me to fall sick. I had quite lost my appetite and was almost reduced to a skeleton. The farmer observed it and, concluding I soon must die, decided to earn as much as possible before I died. While he was thinking these things over, however, a man named Slardal came from Court and ordered my master to carry me to the palace. I was wanted for the entertainment of the Queen of Brobdingnag and her ladies-in-waiting.

Her Majesty and those who attended her were delighted with my **demeanor**.[1] I fell on my knees and begged the honor of kissing her Imperial foot. But this gracious princess held out her little finger towards me, which I hugged in both my arms and put the tip of it with the utmost respect to my lips. She asked me some general questions about my country and my travels, which I answered as well as I could. Then she asked whether I would be content to live at Court. I bowed and humbly answered that I was my master's slave, but if it were up to me, I would be proud to devote my life to Her Majesty's service.

Without delay, she asked my master whether he would sell me at a good price. He, who believed I could not live a month, was ready enough to part with me and demanded a thousand pieces of gold. I then begged the Queen to invite Glumdalclitch to stay with me, so that she could continue to be my nurse and teacher. Her Majesty agreed to my request and easily got the farmer's consent, who was happy to have his daughter received at court. With these business deals ended, my master made his way back home, and I must admit that I was relieved to see him go.

---

[1] **demeanor**—manner; the way in which a person behaves.

Early that same evening, the Queen took me in her own hand and carried me to the King, who had heard nothing about my presence. At first he was **skeptical**[1] and wondered why his time should be wasted by a creature as small as myself. The Queen, who knew her husband as well as he knew himself, sat me down on his hand and instructed me to tell my life story. After just a minute or two, the King found himself captivated by tales of my adventures.

I explained to His Majesty that I came from a country of several million people. Everyone there was my size, and the houses and trees were all in proportion. The King listened carefully to everything I said.

---

[1] **skeptical**—doubtful.

The King and Queen decided that I would stay as long as I cared to. The Queen commanded her cabinet-maker to build a box that might serve me for a bedchamber.[2] The box, which was sixteen feet square and twelve feet high, had windows, a door, and two closets. The board that was the ceiling could be lifted up and down by two hinges and locked at night. The room was quilted on all sides and on the floor and ceiling to prevent any accident from the carelessness of those who carried me.

Eventually, the Queen became so fond of my company that she could not eat without me. I had a table placed on the one at which Her Majesty ate, just at her left elbow, and a chair to sit on. Glumdalclitch stood upon a stool on the floor, near my table, to take care of me. No person ate with the Queen but the two princesses. Her Majesty used to put a bit of meat upon one of my dishes, which I carved for myself, and her **diversion**[3] was to see me eat something so small.

For her part, the Queen (even with her weak stomach) took up in one mouthful as much as a dozen English farmers could eat at a meal, which to me was for some time a very sickening sight. She

---

[2] bedchamber—bedroom.

[3] **diversion**—pleasure; amusement.

would crunch the wing of a bird, bones and all, between her teeth, although it were nine times as large as a full-grown turkey. Once, she put a bit of bread into her mouth as big as two twelve-penny loaves.

It was the custom that every Wednesday the King and Queen would dine together with their children in the apartment of His Majesty. During these meals, the King took great pleasure in talking with me. He asked about the manners, religion, laws, government, and learning of Europe; and I gave him as much information as possible. His understanding was so clear, and his judgment so exact, that he made very wise reflections and observations upon all I said. But, I confess, at times I must have talked too much of my own beloved country, of our trade, of our wars by sea and land, of our **schisms**[4] in religion and parties in the state. He would often ask, in between hearty bursts of laughter, such questions as whether I were a Whig or a Tory.[5] During one of these conversations, he turned to a member of his court and observed

---

[4] **schisms**—divisions within a church.

[5] Whig or a Tory—member of one of the two political parties in England.

how **contemptible**[6] a thing was human grandeur, which could be mimicked by such tiny insects as I. I blushed several times with indignation to hear our noble country, the mistress of arts and arms; the **scourge**[7] of France; the **arbitress**[8] of Europe; the seat of virtue, **piety**,[9] honor, and truth; the pride and envy of the world, so badly treated. But I was in no position to resent injuries or insults, so, on thinking about it, I wondered if what he said was not true.

When the Queen placed me on her hand so that I could see ourselves in the mirror, the difference in our size made me look ridiculous.

When the Queen placed me on her hand so that I could see ourselves in the mirror, the difference in our size made me look ridiculous.

There were, however, some things that I could never get used to in this land of giants. For one, nothing angered and **mortified**[10] me so much as the Queen's dwarf. Being of the smallest size that was ever seen in that country, the dwarf became arrogant at seeing a creature so much beneath him.

---

[6] **contemptible**—not worthy of respect; lowly.

[7] **scourge**—cause of severe suffering or punishment.

[8] **arbitress**—decision maker.

[9] **piety**—devotion to God.

[10] **mortified**—humiliated; greatly embarrassed.

He would always swagger and try to look big as he passed by me. One day at dinner, this nasty little cub was so bothered by something I had said to him that, raising himself upon the frame of Her Majesty's chair, he took me up by the middle, let me drop into a large silver bowl of cream, and then ran away as fast as he could. I fell over and, if I had not been a good swimmer, it might have gone very hard with me. But my little nurse ran to my aid and took me out, after I had swallowed more than a quart of cream.

He took me up by the middle, let me drop into a large silver bowl of cream, and then ran away as fast as he could.

Luckily, my only damage was the loss of a suit of clothes, which was utterly spoiled. The dwarf was soundly whipped, and as a further punishment, forced to drink up the bowl of cream into which he had thrown me.

Before that, he had played a nasty trick on me. His trick had set the Queen laughing, although at the same time she was irritated and would have immediately imprisoned him if I had not been so generous as to **intercede**.[11] Her Majesty had taken a marrow bone upon her plate and, after knocking

---

[11] **intercede**—plead on another's behalf.

out the marrow, placed the bone again in the dish upright as it stood before. When she turned her head away, the dwarf took me up in both hands and, squeezing my legs together, pushed them into the marrow bone above my waist. There I was stuck for some time and made a very ridiculous figure. I believe it was near a minute before anyone knew what was become of me, for I was too embarrassed to cry out. But, as the bone was not hot, my legs were not burned, only my stockings and **breeches**[12] were in a sad condition. I asked that the dwarf have no other punishment than a sound whipping.

I was frequently scolded by the Queen because of my fearfulness, and she used to ask me whether the people of my country were as great cowards as myself. I remember one morning when Glumdalclitch had set me in my box upon a window sill, as she usually did on nice days to give me air. After opening my window, I sat down at my table to eat a piece of sweet cake for my breakfast. Suddenly, more than twenty wasps, who were as large as crows, came flying into the room, humming louder than the noise of as many

---

[12] **breeches**—trousers.

bagpipes. Some of them seized my cake and carried it away. Others flew about my head and face, scaring me with the noise and putting me in the utmost terror of their stings. However, I had the courage to rise, draw my sword, and attack them in the air. I killed four of them, but the rest got away, and I shut my window. I carefully saved the stingers of the wasps I killed, and upon my return to England, gave three to a university and kept the fourth for myself.

Besides the large box in which I usually slept, the Queen ordered a smaller one to be made for me, about twelve feet square and ten feet high. This box was to be used for traveling. There were windows on three sides and on the fourth were two strong hooks, so that the box could be hung on the belt loop of the person who carried me during long journeys. These trips in my box gave me the opportunity to see something of the countryside. It was quite beautiful, although the trees, grasses, flowers, and other objects of nature were larger than anything I could have imagined.

I would have lived happily enough in that country if my smallness had not exposed me to several ridiculous and troublesome accidents, some of which I shall tell. Glumdalclitch often carried me into the gardens of the court in my smaller box. Sometimes she would take me out of it and hold me in her hand, or set me down to walk. One day, before the dwarf left the Queen, he followed us into those gardens. After my nurse set me down, the troublemaking dwarf shook the apple tree that was directly above my head. A dozen apples, each of them as large as a barrel of beer, came tumbling about my ears. One of them hit me on the back as I happened to stoop and knocked me down flat on my face.

Another day Glumdalclitch left me on a smooth grass plot to amuse myself while she walked at some distance with her own governess.[1] There suddenly fell such a violent shower of hailstones,[2] which were eighteen hundred times as large as European hailstones, that I was immediately struck to the ground. From this accident, I was so bruised from head to foot that I could not go out for ten days.

But a more dangerous accident happened to me another time in the same garden. My little nurse, believing she had put me in a safe place, went to another part of the garden with her governess and some ladies she knew. While she was absent, a small white spaniel belonging to one of the chief gardeners came near the place where I lay. The dog

---

[1] governess—tutor.

[2] hailstones—balls of ice formed in thunderclouds and falling like rain.

came straight up and, taking me in his mouth, ran to his master. Wagging his tail, the dog set me gently on the ground. By good fortune he had been so well taught that I was carried between his teeth without the least hurt. But the poor gardener, who knew me well and had a great kindness for me, was in a terrible fright. He gently took me up in both his hands and asked me how I did. I was so amazed and out of breath that I could not speak a word. In a few minutes I came to myself, and he carried me safe to my little nurse. By this time, she had returned to the place where she left me and was very upset when I did not appear, nor answer when she called. She severely scolded the gardener on account of his dog. But the whole thing was hushed up and never known at court, for the girl was afraid of the Queen's anger. As for me, it was too embarrassing a story to be told.

The Queen often used to hear me talk of my sea voyages and took all occasions to amuse me when I was sad. One day she asked me whether I knew how to handle a sail or an oar and whether a little exercise of rowing might not be good for my health. I answered that I understood both well. So Her Majesty had a tiny boat made that was just the right size for me. Then she had a wooden **trough**[3] made that was three hundred feet long and eighty feet deep. There I would row and practice my seafaring skills, much to the delight of the Queen and her ladies. Sometimes I would put up my sail, and then my business was only to steer, while the ladies made me a **gale**[4] with their fans. When they were tired, some of the pages would blow my sail forward with their breath. When I had done, Glumdalclitch always carried my boat into her closet and hung it on a nail to dry.

Of course, these sea journeys were not without danger. Once, one of the servants, whose job it was to fill my trough every third day with fresh water, was so careless he let a huge frog slip out of his pail. The frog lay hidden till I was put into my boat. Then, seeking a resting place, it climbed up and made the boat lean so much on one side that I was forced to balance it with all my weight on the other to prevent it from overturning.

---

[3] **trough**—long, narrow container for holding water.
[4] **gale**—very strong wind.

The King, who, as I said before, was an intelligent man, would frequently order that I should be brought in my box and set on the table in his room. He would then question me closely about the habits and government of my country. I told his Majesty that our **dominions**[1] consisted of two islands, in which there were three mighty kingdoms under one **sovereign**,[2] beside our plantations in America. I spoke long about the fertility of our soil and the temperature of our climate. I then spoke about the English Parliament, including a long discussion about the House of Peers and the House of Commons.[3] I also gave a long lecture on the history of England and its royal families.

---

[1] **dominions**—territories.

[2] **sovereign**—king, queen, or other ruler.

[3] the House of Peers and the House of Commons—the two houses of the British legislature. The House of Peers (or House of Lords) is the upper, nonelective house of the Parliament of Great Britain. It was composed of nobles and clergymen of high rank. The House of Commons is the lower, elective house of the Parliament.

The King was fascinated by what I told him and took notes as I spoke. He also questioned me carefully about points of government he didn't understand, and I tried to answer these questions as best I could. At times we would disagree upon an issue, and then we would debate the question for hours at a time. He was particularly interested to hear that England kept a standing army at all times, even during times of peace and among a free people. He could not imagine of whom we were afraid, or against whom we were to fight.

He was perfectly astonished with the historical account I gave him of my country's affairs during the last century. He said it sounded like nothing more than a heap of **conspiracies**,[4] rebellions, murders, massacres, and revolutions. It was, he thought, the very worst that greed, hypocrisy, cruelty, rage, madness, hatred, envy, lust, malice, or ambition could produce. His Majesty took me into his hands and, stroking me gently, said these words, which I shall never forget.

"My little friend Grildrig, you have clearly proved that, in your country, ignorance, idleness, and vice may sometimes be the only ingredients for qualifying a legislator and that laws are best

---

[4] **conspiracies**—secret plots.

explained, interpreted, and applied by those whose best interests lie in misusing and avoiding them." He was disgusted, he said, by our cheating nature. He said we were "the most **pernicious**[5] race of **odious**[6] little **vermin**[7] that nature ever suffered to crawl upon the surface of the earth."

Nothing but an extreme love of truth could have stopped me from hiding this part of the story. But I must say that I avoided many of his questions and gave each point a much more favorable turn than the strictness of truth would allow. I sincerely tried to hide my country's weaknesses and light up her virtues and beauties. Unfortunately, I was not successful in my many talks with His Majesty.

> *I avoided many of his questions and gave each point a much more favorable turn than the strictness of truth would allow.*

---

[5] **pernicious**—destructive; evil.

[6] **odious**—disgusting.

[7] **vermin**—destructive insects and small animals, such as fleas, lice, and rats.

Hoping to gain His Majesty's favor and shed a positive light on England, I told him of an invention discovered between three and four hundred years ago. I explained that a type of explosive powder could be rammed into a hollow tube of brass or iron and with the smallest spark of fire could drive a ball of iron or lead with enough force that an entire army rank could be destroyed at one time. The largest balls, I explained, could batter the strongest walls to the ground or sink a ship with a thousand men aboard. This information I humbly offered to His Majesty to show how much I appreciated his **hospitality.**[1] Furthermore, I would be happy to show His Majesty's people how to create machines such as this, which could kill or wound so easily and quickly.

---

[1] **hospitality**—generous treatment of guests or strangers.

The King was horrified at the description I had given of this invention and was doubly horrified by my proposal to show his people the technology. He was amazed that such **groveling**[2] insects as we could entertain such inhuman practices. How could we be so unmoved by the scenes of blood and destruction that were a direct result of the use of these machines? He finished by saying that he would rather lose half his kingdom than be given the knowledge of how to make such a machine. With that, he commanded me to say no more of the topic. This showed a strange effect of narrow principles and short views! The King, who had great wisdom and learning, and who was loved by his subjects, would allow such an opportunity to slip out of his hands! He could have been absolute master of the lives, liberties, and fortunes of his people.

He was amazed that such groveling insects as we could entertain such inhuman practices.

At all times, no matter how comfortable I was, I always kept with me a strong desire to return to my homeland. Unfortunately, I had no idea how I

[2] **groveling**—acting in a lowly manner; crawling in fear and humility.

might accomplish this, as the ship in which I sailed was the first ever seen on that coast.

For the most part, I was treated with great kindness. I was the favorite of a great King and Queen and the delight of the whole court. But it was an unpleasant kind of delight—and one not appropriate for a human being. I felt like a well-cared-for pet.

I had now been two years in this country. Around the beginning of the third year, Glumdalclitch and I attended the King and Queen in a journey to the south coast of the kingdom. I was carried, as usual, in my traveling box. As I have already described, it was a very convenient room about twelve feet wide.

When we came to our journey's end, the King thought it proper to pass a few days at his palace near Flanflasnic, a city within eighteen miles of the seaside. Glumdalclitch and I were tired. I had a small cold, but the poor girl was so ill that she could not get up from bed. I longed to see the ocean, which would be the scene of my escape, if ever it should happen. I pretended to be worse than I really was and asked permission to take the fresh air of the sea. I went with a page whom I was

I longed to see the ocean, which would be the scene of my escape, if ever it should happen.

very fond of, and who had sometimes been trusted with me. I shall never forget with what unwillingness Glumdalclitch agreed, nor the strict orders she gave the page to be careful of me, bursting at the same time into a flood of tears, as if she had some **foreboding**[3] of what was to happen.

The boy took me out in my box about half an hour's walk from the palace, towards the rocks on the seashore. I ordered him to set me down and told him that I would take a nap. The boy closed my windows tight to keep out the cold, and I soon fell asleep. I think that at this point the boy, thinking no danger could happen, went away to the rocks to look for birds' eggs or some such thing.

In any event, I found myself suddenly awakened by a jolt to the ring which was fastened to the top of the box. I felt my box raised very high in the air, and then I felt it moved forward at a tremendous speed. The first jolt had almost shaken me out of my hammock, but afterwards the motion was easy enough. I called out several times as loud as I could, but there was no one to hear. I looked towards my windows and could see nothing but

---

[3] **foreboding**—strong feeling that there will be a future misfortune.

the clouds and sky. I heard a noise just over my head like the clapping of wings, and then began to understand the frightening situation I was in. It was clear that some eagle or other large bird had got the ring of my box in his beak. He probably intended to let the box fall on a rock, like a tortoise in a shell, so that he could pick out my body and eat it.

Soon I noticed that the flutter of wings increased. My box was tossed up and down, like a signpost on a windy day. I heard several bangs, and then all of a sudden felt myself falling straight down for more than a minute, but with such incredible swiftness that I almost lost my breath. My fall was stopped by a terrible splash, after which I was quite in the dark for another minute. Then my box began to rise so high that I could see light from the tops of my windows. I found that I had fallen into the sea and that the box was now floating.

I found that I had fallen into the sea and that the box was now floating.

How often did I then wish myself with my dear Glumdalclitch! I could not stop myself from feeling terrible about my poor nurse and the grief she would suffer because I was gone. I knew also the

Queen would be very angry and was likely to punish the boy severely for his simple mistake.

With nothing left to do, I opened the window that was closest to the ceiling, climbed onto a chair, and began yelling out the window in the loudest voice I could manage. I called and called until I was almost hoarse. Then I had the idea of waving a handkerchief on a stick out the window. Each time the waves pushed my box high into the air, I waved my stick and called loudly in the hopes that I would be sighted.

I waved my stick and called loudly in the hopes that I would be sighted.

At last I heard a noise like that of a cable, grating as it passed through a ring. I then found that I was hoisted at least three feet higher than I was before. I now heard steps over my head, and somebody calling through the hole with a loud voice in English: "If there be anybody below, let them speak." I answered that I was an Englishman, drawn by ill fortune into the greatest disaster that ever any creature underwent. I begged to be delivered out of the prison I was in. The voice replied that I was safe, for my box was fastened to their ship, and the carpenter would come and saw a hole in the cover, large enough to pull me out.

I answered that that was unnecessary. All that was needed was for one of the crew to put his finger in the ring at the top of the box and take the box out of the sea and onto the ship. Some of them upon hearing me talk so wildly thought I was mad. Others laughed, for indeed it never came into my head that I was now among people of my own size and strength. The carpenter came and in a few minutes sawed a passage about four feet square. He then let down a small ladder for me to climb, and from there I was taken into the ship in a very weak condition.

The sailors were all amazed and asked me a thousand questions. I was equally surprised at the sight of so many **pygmies,**[4] for this is how I thought of them, after having so long accustomed my eyes to the monstrous creatures I had left. The Captain, Mr. Thomas Wilcocks, observed I was about to faint, so he took me into his cabin, gave me a brandy, and then insisted I take a little rest.

I slept some hours, but I was disturbed with dreams of the place I had left and the dangers I had escaped. Upon waking, however, I found

[4] **pygmies**—people of unusually small size.

myself much recovered. It was now about eight o'clock at night, and the Captain ordered supper immediately, thinking I had already been without food for too long. He treated me with great kindness and asked me to tell him of my adventures. I told him the story in bits and pieces, stopping as needed for rest and refreshment.

No matter how much I tried to convince him otherwise, the Captain felt certain that my brain was disturbed. He promised to get me safely to the nearest port where I could get the help I needed. I begged his patience to hear my story again, and slowly he became convinced of my truthfulness. To further confirm my story, I showed him the few things that I had collected in the land of the giants. There was a collection of needles and pins from a foot to two feet long, four wasp-stingers, which were close to a foot in length, some of the Queen's hair, and a gold ring, which Her Majesty had given me to wear over my head as a collar. Lastly, I desired him to see the pants I had on, which were made of a mouse's skin.

Once he understood the truth, he encouraged me to tell the world by writing of my adventures. My reply was that I thought we had too many books of travels, but I thanked him for his good opinion.

After several more weeks at sea, the Captain was able to dock at a British port on June 3, 1706, about nine months after my escape. I offered to leave my goods as a form of payment for carrying me as a passenger, but the Captain did not want one penny. We took kind leave of each other, and I made him promise he would come to see me at my house in Redriff. I hired a horse and guide for five shillings, which I borrowed from the Captain.

As I was on the road, I observed the smallness of the houses, trees, cattle, and people. I began to feel like I was back in Lilliput, afraid of trampling on every traveler I met. I often called aloud to have people stand out of the way, so that I came close to having a broken head for my rudeness.

When I came to my own house, I bent down to go in (like a goose under a gate) for fear of striking my head. My wife ran out to embrace me, but I stooped lower than her knees, thinking she could otherwise never be able to reach my mouth. My daughter kneeled to ask my blessing, but I could not see her till she arose. I had been used to standing with my head and eyes looking to above sixty feet for so long. Then I went to take her up with one hand, by the waist. I looked down upon the servants and one or two friends who were in the house, as if they had been pygmies, and I a giant. In short, I behaved in such a strange manner that they all concluded I had lost my mind.

In a little time, however, I and my family and friends came to an understanding of what I had experienced. My wife insisted I should never go to sea any more, but I knew that would be impossible, as the reader will soon know. In the meantime, I here end the second part of my unfortunate voyages.

THE END OF THE SECOND PART

A Voyage to Laputa, Balnibarbi, Glubbdubdrib, and Luggnagg

PART THREE, CHAPTER ONE

I had not been at home more than ten days when Captain William Robinson, Commander of the *Hope-well*, a stout ship of three hundred tons, came to my house. After asking about my health, he told me that he intended to make a voyage to the East Indies in two months and that he would like me to be surgeon of the ship. He offered me double the salary that I would usually earn on such a trip.

I could not reject his proposal. The thirst I had of seeing the world was as violent as ever, even though I had suffered so many mishaps. The only difficulty that remained was to persuade my wife, whose **consent**[1] I at last obtained.

We set out on August 5, 1706, and arrived at Fort St. George on April 11, 1707. We stayed there three weeks to refresh our crew, many of whom

---

[1] **consent**—agreement; permission.

were sick. From there we went to Tonquin, where the Captain decided to stay some time because many of the goods he intended to buy were not yet ready. So he bought a sloop[2] and loaded it with various goods that the Tonquinese trade with neighboring islands. He appointed me master of the sloop and told me to trade for two months.

On the tenth day, we were chased by two pirate ships, which soon overtook us.

We had not sailed more than three days when a great storm arose. We were driven five days to the north-northeast, and then to the east. After that, we had fair weather. On the tenth day, we were chased by two pirate ships, which soon overtook us. Because the sloop carried so many goods, she was low in the water and sailed slowly. We were boarded first by two pirates, who entered furiously at the head of a large group of men. When they found us all lying upon our faces (as I ordered), they tied us up with strong ropes, set a guard upon us, and went to search the ship.

I observed among them a Dutchman, who seemed to be of some authority, though he was not

---

[2] sloop—small sailboat with one mast and two sails.

commander of either ship. As I spoke Dutch fairly well, I was able to tell him who we were and begged him to take pity on us. The Dutchman refused to listen and threatened to kill us all.

The Dutchman refused to listen and threatened to kill us all.

The largest of the two pirate ships was commanded by a Japanese Captain, who spoke a little Dutch. He came up to me, and after several questions, which I answered in great humility, he said we should not die. I made the Captain a very low bow, and then, turning to the Dutchman, said that I was relieved to find at least one man with some mercy. But I had soon reason to be sorry I said those foolish words. That cruel man, having decided that I would cause more trouble than he was prepared to deal with, worked to convince the others that I should be thrown into the sea. Fortunately, the Japanese Captain had promised he would not kill me, so the men devised a plan whereby I would be set adrift in a canoe with four days' worth of food and water.

The rest of my crew was divided into both pirate ships to await their fate. As to myself, the pirates prepared a small boat with paddles, sail, and food. I got down into the canoe, while the

Dutchman cursed me from up on the deck. The pirates lowered the boat none too gently into the water, and I was off on my own once again.

When I had paddled some distance from the pirates, I discovered by my pocket glass[3] several islands to the southeast. I set up my sail, the wind being fair, with a plan to reach the nearest of those islands, which I was able to do in about three hours. Once I landed on the nearest island, I found that it was all rocky. I was able to get many birds' eggs, which I roasted over a small fire. I passed the night under the shelter of a rock and slept pretty well.

The next day I sailed to another island, and then to a third and fourth, sometimes using my sail and sometimes my paddles. But not to trouble the reader with the details of my troubles, let it be enough to state that on the fifth day I arrived at the last island in my sight, which lay south-southeast to the former. This island was farther than I expected. I circled almost around it before I could find a convenient place to land, which was a small creek about three times the width of my canoe. I

---

[3] pocket glass—small telescope.

found the island to be all rocky, with only a few tufts of grass and sweet-smelling herbs. I took out my small amount of food and, after having refreshed myself, stored the remaining part in a cave. I gathered plenty of eggs upon the rocks and got a quantity of dry seaweed and dry grass for a fire. I lay all night in the cave where I had put my food. My bed was the same dry grass and seaweed that I intended to use for fuel. I slept very little, for my worries **prevailed over**[4] my weariness and kept me awake.

The next morning, I found myself so depressed that I could not rise. It was near noon when I finally crept out of my cave. I walked awhile among the rocks. The sky was perfectly clear, and the sun so hot that I was forced to turn my face from it. All of a sudden it became much darker. I looked up and saw a vast **opaque**[5] body between me and the sun. It seemed to be perhaps two miles high and was so large that it hid the sun for six or seven minutes. It appeared to be of a firm substance, with a bottom that was flat, smooth, and shining very bright from

[4] **prevailed over**—were stronger than.
[5] **opaque**—not allowing light to pass through.

the reflection of the sea below. I took out my pocket glass and could plainly see many people moving up and down the sides of it, which appeared to be sloping. From this distance, however, I could not tell what any of the people were doing.

I was ready to hope that this floating island might in some way or another help to deliver me from the **desolate**[6] place and condition I was in. But at the same time, the reader can hardly imagine my astonishment at seeing an island in the air, inhabited by men who were able to move the island up, down, or forward.

The reader can hardly imagine my astonishment at seeing an island in the air, inhabited by men who were able to move the island up, down, or forward.

I stood still for quite a while, observing the island and the direction it took. When it moved close to where I was, I raised my cap in the air, waved it wildly, and called out in the loudest voice I could. Almost immediately, I saw a crowd gather at the side that was most in my view. They clearly had discovered me, although they made no reply to my shouting.

---

[6] **desolate**—uninhabited and lonely.

Quickly, the number of people increased, and in less than half an hour the island was moved and raised in such a manner that the lowest gallery was less than a hundred yards from where I stood. I then put myself into the most **supplicating**[7] positions and spoke in the humblest accent, but received no answer.

Those who stood just above me seemed by their dress to be persons of distinction. They spoke earnestly with each other, looking often upon me. At length one of them called out in a clear, polite, smooth dialect that sounded like Italian; and therefore I returned an answer in that language, hoping at least that the **cadence**[8] might be agreeable to his ears. Although neither of us understood the other, my meaning was easily known, for the people saw the trouble I was in.

They made signs for me to come down from the rock and go towards the shore, which I did. The flying island was then raised to a convenient height and a chain was let down from the lowest gallery. A seat was fastened to the bottom of the chain, so I sat down and was drawn up by ropes.

---

[7] **supplicating**—pleading.

[8] **cadence**—rise and fall of a person's voice.

As soon as I landed, I was surrounded by
a crowd of people. Never have I seen a race of
people so strange in their shapes, habits, and faces.
Their heads were all tilted either to the right or
the left. One of their eyes turned inward, and the
other directly up to the sky. Their outer garments
were decorated with the figures of suns, moons,
and stars, interwoven with those of fiddles, flutes,
harps, trumpets, guitars, and many other musical
instruments. Here and there I saw many who
appeared to be servants, each of whom carried a
balloon fastened to a short stick. In each balloon
was a small quantity of dried peas or little pebbles
(as I was afterwards told). With these balloons they
now and then flapped the mouths and ears of those
who stood near them. It seems that the people are
so involved with their thoughts that they neither

can speak nor listen without feeling something on their ears or mouth. Later I learned that this was true and that those who could afford to keep at least one flapper as a servant never go out unless the flapper is along. The business of the flapper, when there are two or more people, is to gently strike with the balloon the mouth of the person who is to speak and the ear of those who are spoken to.

In short order, the crowd of people took me to the stairs and from there to the royal palace. While we were walking, they forgot several times what they were doing and left me to myself until their attention was again roused by their flappers.

At last we entered the palace and proceeded into a grand **chamber**,[1] where I saw a King seated on his throne, attended on each side by several persons in fine clothes. On the table in front of the throne was a set of globes, spheres, and mathematical instruments of all kinds. The King was deeply involved in some mathematical problem and attended to it for at least an hour before he was able to solve it. On either side of him stood a young servant, each with a flap in his hands.

---

[1] **chamber**—room.

Whenever they saw the King's attention wander, one of them gently struck his mouth, and the other his right ear. At this, the King started like one awakened from a deep sleep.

When His Majesty finally noticed that we were in his presence, he spoke a few words. As he was speaking, a young man with a flap came up to me and flapped me gently on

As he was speaking, a young man with a flap came up to me and flapped me gently on the right ear.

the right ear. I made signs, as well as I could, that I had no need for such an instrument. I found out later that this refusal gave the King and the whole court a very negative opinion of my ability to understand. The King asked me several questions, and I answered him in all the languages I had. When it was found that I could neither understand nor be understood, I was taken to a room in the King's palace, where I was to await further instructions. My dinner was brought, and four persons of quality, whom I remembered I saw very near the King's person, did me the honor to dine with me. We had two courses of three dishes each. In the first course there was a shoulder of **mutton**[2] cut into an **equilateral triangle**,[3] a piece of beef cut into a **rhomboid**,[4] and a pudding cut into a **cycloid**.[5] The second course was two ducks, shaped in the form of fiddles; sausages and puddings resembling flutes; and a breast of veal in the shape of a harp. The servants cut our bread into cones, cylinders, **parallelograms**,[6] and several other geometric figures.

The servants cut our bread into cones, cylinders, parallelograms, and several other geometric figures.

While we were at dinner, I made bold to ask the names of several things in their language. The noble persons, with the assistance of their flappers, were delighted to give me answers, hoping to make me admire their great abilities. I was soon able to call for bread and drink or whatever else I wanted.

After dinner my company left, and a person was sent to me by the King's order, attended by a flapper. He brought with him pen, ink, and paper, and three or four books. He showed by signs that he was sent to teach me the language. We sat

---

[2] **mutton**—the cooked flesh of fully grown sheep.

[3] **equilateral triangle**—triangle with equal sides. ▲

[4] **rhomboid**—parallelogram with unequal adjacent sides. ◢

[5] **cycloid**—circular shape. ●

[6] **parallelograms**—four-sided plane figures with opposite sides that are parallel. ▰

together four hours, in which time I wrote down a great number of words in columns, with the translations over against them. He showed me also in one of his books the figures of the sun, moon, and stars, the zodiac, the tropics, and polar circles, together with the **denominations**[7] of many figures of planes and solids. He gave me the names and descriptions of all the musical instruments and the general terms of art in playing on each of them. After he had left me, I placed all my words with their translations in alphabetical order. And thus in a few days, by the help of a very good memory, I started to understand their language. I found out that this place was called Laputa. I interpret this as the Flying or Floating Island.

The King's servants, who saw that my clothes were tattered, ordered that a tailor be brought to my rooms. He came the next morning and measured me for a suit of clothes. He did so by computing my weight, height, and density. He then used a ruler and compasses to describe the outlines of my whole body all on paper. In six days he brought me a new suit of clothes, which were

---

[7] **denominations**—values or sizes.

very ill-made and quite out of shape. Probably he had made a mistake in his calculations. I realized this was why so many of the people on Laputa had ill-fitting clothes.

Over the next several days, I worked on enlarging my vocabulary. The next time I went to court, I was able to understand many of the things that the King said and was able to reply to some of his questions. His Majesty had given orders that the island should move northeast to a point over Lagado, which was the capital of the kingdom below, upon the firm earth. It was about ninety leagues[8] away, and our voyage lasted four days and a half. I was unable to feel any movement at all.

In our journey towards Lagado, His Majesty ordered that the island should stop over certain towns and villages, so that he might receive the **petitions**[9] of his subjects. To do this, several threads were let down with small weights at the bottom. On these threads the people strung their questions and watched them being pulled up to the island. Sometimes we received wine and food from below, which were drawn up by ropes.

---

[8] ninety leagues—about 270 miles.

[9] **petitions**—requests.

The knowledge I had in mathematics and music helped me to learn their language, which relied much upon science and music. Their ideas were expressed mostly in lines and figures. If they would, for example, praise the beauty of a woman, or any other animal, they would describe it in geometrical terms or by musical terms.

But the Laputans, no matter how intellectually gifted, are quite lacking in practical matters. Their houses are not at all well built, their food is not well prepared and, as I have said, their clothes are ill fitting. They are also poor reasoners and given to any form of opposition, unless they happen to have the right answer, which seldom happens. Not surprisingly, they have no imagination or invention.

They worry that the Earth will be destroyed somehow—absorbed or swallowed up, perhaps, by the sun.

Furthermore, these people never enjoy a minute's peace of mind. They are always worried about dangers that might befall them. They can neither sleep quietly in their beds nor have any enjoyment of the common pleasures or amusements of life. In particular, they worry that the Earth will be destroyed somehow—absorbed or swallowed up, perhaps, by the sun. Then they worry that the face of the sun will stop giving light to the world. They worry that the sun, having no food, will be used up. When they would meet an acquaintance in the morning, the first question was always about the sun's health, how it looked at its setting and rising, and whether there were any comets about.

In contrast, the women of the island are very **vivacious**.[10] They ignore their husbands and are very fond of strangers. The wives and daughters **lament**[11] that they have to stay on the floating island, although I think it the most delicious spot of ground in the world. Although they live here in the greatest plenty and are allowed to do whatever they please, they long to see the world. I was told about a great court lady, who has several children. She is married to the prime minister, who is very fond of her, and she lives in the finest palace on the island. She went down to Lagado, pretending to be ill, and hid herself there for several months. Finally, the King sent for her. She was found in a run-down eating-house all in rags, having sold her

---

[10] **vivacious**—lively.

[11] **lament**—show sorrow or grief for.

clothes. And although her husband received her back with all possible kindness and without the least anger, she soon after managed to steal down again with all her jewels and has not been heard of since.

After I understood more of the Laputan language, I asked permission to see some of the parts of the island. I was told that I would be free to roam. I discovered that the Floating Island is exactly circular,[1] with a diameter of four and one-half miles. It is three hundred yards thick. A magnet moves it up and down, depending upon its attraction to Balnibarbi, the island above which it floats.

The King rules Laputa and Balnibarbi, although there is often tension between the Laputans and the Balnibarbians. The King and his ministry are eager to enslave the Balnibarbians and rule them **absolutely.**[2] The Balnibarbians, of course, object to

---

[1] circular—round like a circle.

[2] **absolutely**—without limits or restrictions.

this idea. When a town in Balnibarbi rebels, the King has two methods of forcing the people to obey. The first and the mildest course is to keep Laputa hovering over the area, so that the town will not have sun and rain. And if the crime deserves it, the town is at the same time pelted from above with great stones. The people have no defense against the attack but to creep into cellars or caves while the roofs of their houses are destroyed. If the people continue to be stubborn, or raise revolts, his last remedy is to let the Floating Island drop directly upon their heads, causing destruction of both houses and men. This is an extreme measure that the King prefers not to use, and his advisors, who all have estates below, never recommend it.

Although I cannot say that I was ill treated on this island, I must confess I thought myself too much ignored, in a rather **contemptuous**[3] way. Neither the King nor the people appeared to be curious about anything except mathematics and music, in which subjects I was inferior and, for this reason, I was not respected.

---

[3] **contemptuous**—disrespectful.

On the other hand, after having seen all the parts of the island, I was very eager to leave it, as I was tired of those people. They were indeed excellent in two sciences for which I have great regard; but at the same time they were so abstracted and involved in thinking that I never met with such disagreeable companions. I spoke only with women, tradesmen, flappers, and court pages during the two months of my stay there. I felt these were the only people from whom I could ever receive a reasonable answer. This habit of avoiding all mathematical conversations gave me an even worse reputation with the **intellectuals**[4] on the island.

For these reasons and more, I decided to leave this island at the first opportunity. I begged His Majesty for permission to depart. After much discussion, the King decided in my favor, and I left the Floating Island on February 16. The king gave me a gift of money and, without much ceremony, I was lowered to the island of Balnibarbi, near Lagado.

Upon arriving, I was happy to find myself on firm ground once again. I made my way to the home of a great lord, whose name was Munodi.

---

[4] **intellectuals**—people who rely more on thinking than on emotion or feeling; scholars.

I stayed with Munodi during my visit, and was entertained in a most hospitable manner.

The morning after my arrival, Munodi took me in his **chariot**[5] to see the town, which is about half the size of London. The houses are very oddly built and most of them in need of repair. The people in the streets walked fast and

The people in the streets walked fast and looked wild, and their clothes were generally in rags.

looked wild, and their clothes were generally in rags. Then we went about three miles into the country, where I saw many laborers working with several sorts of tools in the ground, but I was not able to guess what they were doing. I did not see any sign of corn or grass, although the soil appeared to be excellent. I asked Munodi what could be meant by so many busy heads, hands, and faces, both in the streets and the fields, because I could not discover any good effects they produced. I had never seen (I told him) a soil so poorly **cultivated**,[6] houses so poorly built, or a people whose faces and behavior showed so much misery and want.

Lord Munodi replied that I had not been long enough among them to form a judgment and that

---

[5] **chariot**—horse-drawn carriage.

[6] **cultivated**—prepared for growing crops.

the different nations of the world had different customs. But when we returned to his palace, he asked me how I liked the building, what absurdities I had observed, and what quarrel I had with the dress or looks of his servants. This he could safely do, because everything about him was magnificent, regular, and polite. I answered that His Excellency's **prudence,**[7] quality, and fortune had protected him from the defects I saw out on the street and fields. He then said that if I would go with him to his country house, about twenty miles distant, there would be more time for this kind of conversation. I replied that I would go as he wished. The next morning we set out.

During our journey, he showed me the several methods used by farmers in managing their lands, which to me were completely impossible to understand. Except in some very few places, I could not see one ear of corn or blade of grass. But in three hours' traveling the scene was wholly changed. We came into a most beautiful country; farmers' houses at small distances, neatly built; the fields enclosed, containing vineyards, grain

---

[7] **prudence**—careful management.

fields, and meadows. Never do I remember a more delightful scene. His Excellency observed my reaction, and told me with a sigh that there his estate began, where the grass was green and the houses were so pleasing to the eye. His fellow countrymen ridiculed and despised him for managing his affairs no better and for setting so bad an example to the entire kingdom.

When I asked him to explain what he meant, he thought for a moment and told me the following story. About forty years ago, certain persons went up to Laputa, either upon business or entertainment, and after five months they came back with a **smattering**[8] of knowledge in mathematics. These people began to dislike the management of everything below and fell into changing the way people think about all arts, sciences, languages, and mechanics. They made new rules and methods of agriculture and building and new instruments and tools for all trades and manufactures. Unfortunately, none of these projects and experiments has been perfected, and, in the meantime, the whole country lies miserably wasted. The houses are in ruins and the people are without decent food or clothes.

---

[8] **smattering**—small amount.

After hearing his story, I thought for a moment and then asked the obvious: why was his estate so well-maintained, his house so finely built, and his clothes so elegant and well-constructed? With a sigh, he replied that he was not **enterprising**[9] and was happy to continue the habits of his ancestors. For this reason, he was ridiculed and criticized.

For the next several weeks I toured Balnibarbi. All around me I saw failed experiments. Upon the recommendation of my host, I visited the Grand Academy, which is home to the many experiments and scientific trials that so fascinate the Balnibarbians. In one room of the Academy, I watched as a scientist tried to take sunbeams from a cucumber so that he might supply the King's garden with heat whenever it was needed. He had been working on this project for eight years. In another room, I saw a noted scientist attempt to reduce human **excrement**[10] to its original food. He had a weekly allowance

I watched as a scientist tried to extract sunbeams from a cucumber.

---

[9] **enterprising**—showing energy and initiative.
[10] **excrement**—waste products of the body; dung.

from the Society and a barrel filled to the top with human waste. I saw another man at work in an attempt to turn ice into gunpowder.

The more experiments and projects I saw, the more **disillusioned**[11] I became. These were fools of the highest order, I thought to myself. Because of this, I decided the time was right to go. To be truthful, I saw nothing in this country that could invite me to a longer visit, and began to think of returning home to England.

---

[11] **disillusioned**—freed from false ideas. Gulliver means he lost respect for scholarly activities.

My understanding of world geography helped me to make a brilliant plan for returning home. Balnibarbi, I knew, extended eastward toward an unknown tract of America, west of California, and north of the Pacific Ocean. Approximately 150 miles from Lagado, there is a good port on the great island of Luggnagg. Luggnagg stands southeastward of Japan, which is approximately 300 miles distant. There is a strict **alliance**[1] between the Japanese Emperor and the King of Luggnagg, which makes it easy to sail from one island to the other. I decided therefore to direct my course this way, so that I might eventually return to Europe. I hired two mules with a guide to show me the way and to carry my small baggage.

---

[1] **alliance**—treaty of friendship.

I took leave of Munodi, who had shown me so much kindness and who made me a generous present at my departure.

My journey was without accident or adventure. When I arrived at the port of Maldonada (a town on the way toward Luggnagg), there was no ship in the harbor bound for Luggnagg, nor likely to be one for some time. I soon met some people, however, and was very hospitably received. A gentleman told me that since the ships bound for Luggnagg could not be ready in less than a month, it might be enjoyable for me to take a trip to the little island of Glubbdubdrib, about 15 miles off to the southwest. He offered himself and a friend to accompany me.

Glubbdubdrib, as nearly as I can interpret the word, means the Island of Sorcerers or Magicians. It is about one-third as large as the Isle of Wight[2] and extremely fruitful. It is governed by the head of a certain tribe whose members are all magicians. Members of this tribe marry only among each other, and the oldest person is Governor.

The Governor and his family are helped by servants of a kind that is somewhat unusual. By his skill in **necromancy**,[3] the Governor has the

---

[2] Isle of Wight—small island off the southern coast of England.

[3] **necromancy**—communicating with the spirits of the dead in order to predict the future.

power to call whom he pleases from the dead and command their service for twenty-four hours, but no longer.

When we arrived at the island, one of the gentlemen who accompanied me went to the Governor. He asked admittance for a stranger who came on purpose to have the honor of visiting His Highness. This was immediately granted. We all three entered the gate of the palace between two rows of guards, who were all armed and dressed in a very strange manner. In fact, something in their faces made my flesh creep with a horror I cannot express. We passed through several rooms till we came to the royal chamber. There, after three deep bows and a few general questions, we were permitted to sit on three stools near the lowest step of His Highness's throne. He understood the language of Balnibarbi, although it was different from that of his island. He asked me to give him some account of my travels. To let me see that I should be treated without ceremony, he dismissed all his attendants with a snap of his finger. To my great astonishment, they vanished in an instant, like visions in a dream.

Something in their faces made my flesh creep with a horror I cannot express.

I could not recover myself from this sight for some time, till the Governor assured me that I should not be hurt. Then I began to take courage and told His Highness a short history of my adventures. Later, I had the honor to dine with the Governor, where a new set of ghosts served up the meat and waited on the table. I was now less frightened than I had been in the morning. I stayed till sunset but humbly desired his Highness to excuse me for not accepting his invitation to spend the night. The next morning, we returned to pay a visit to the Governor.

We stayed on this island for ten days and spent almost every day with the Governor. I soon grew so used to the sight of spirits that the third or fourth time they gave me no emotion at all. For entertainment, the Governor invited me to call up whatever persons I would choose to name, from the beginning of the world to the present time, and then to ask them any questions I wanted to ask. There was only one condition—my questions must be about the times they lived in. I might be sure that they would tell me the truth, he said, for lying was impossible in the lower world.

I humbly thanked His Highness for so great an opportunity. My first idea was to call up a scene of pomp and magnificence, so I asked to see Alexander the Great,[4] at the head of his army just after the battle of Arbela. The Governor snapped his fingers, and there appeared Alexander himself. It was with great difficulty that I understood his Greek, as I spoke so little Greek myself.

> *The Governor snapped his fingers, and there appeared Alexander himself.*

He assured me upon his honor that he was not poisoned, but had died of a fever caused by too much drinking.

Next I saw Hannibal[5] passing the Alps, who told me he had had not a drop of vinegar in his camp. Then I asked to see Caesar and Brutus.[6] I was struck with a profound **veneration**[7] at the sight of Brutus, and could easily have spent months in

---

[4] Alexander the Great—The King of Macedonia from 336 to 323 B.C., Alexander conquered the Greek city-states and the whole Persian empire, which extended to Egypt.

[5] Hannibal—The Carthaginian general who terrified Rome during the Second Punic War, Hannibal is remembered for the extremely difficult crossing he and his troops made through the Alps in 221 B.C. Some say Hannibal's soldiers became unruly after consuming huge amounts of vinegar, a fermented alcohol.

[6] Caesar and Brutus—A brilliant general and politician, Julius Caesar became the dictator of Rome. In 44 B.C., a group led by Brutus stabbed Caesar at a meeting of the Roman Senate on March 15 (the Ides of March).

[7] **veneration**—respect.

deep discussion with him. The next day, I asked for Aristotle[8] and Homer[9] and other philosophers who explained their systems to Aristotle. I called up various kings, queens, and princes of the English blood line and found some to be quite different from the ways they were described in my school-boy textbooks.

Because every person I asked to see looked exactly the same as he had when he was alive, it gave me sad reflections to observe how sturdy they all looked in comparison to the English men and women of today. How the race of humankind had **degenerated**[10] over these last hundred years! The **pox**[11] had altered every aspect of the English face, shortened the size of the bodies, unbraced the nerves, relaxed the muscles, introduced a **sallow**[12] complexion, and rendered the flesh loose and **rancid**.[13]

> *How the race of humankind had degenerated over these last hundred years!*

---

[8] Aristotle—A Greek philosopher who lived from 384 to 322 B.C., Aristotle developed formal, deductive logic.

[9] Homer—The great epic poet of ancient Greece, Homer is the earliest known poet in European literature.

[10] **degenerated**—worsened, declined.

[11] **pox**—slang for syphilis, a life-threatening venereal disease that killed hundreds of thousands of men and women during the seventeenth, eighteenth, and nineteenth centuries.

[12] **sallow**—sickly yellowish color.

[13] **rancid**—stale, unpleasantly smelly; nasty.

The day of our departure for Luggnagg
having come, I took leave of the Governor of
Glubbdubdrib. I returned with my two companions
to Maldonada where, after two weeks of waiting,
a ship was ready to sail for Luggnagg. The two
gentlemen, and some others, were so generous
and kind as to give me supplies and see me on
board. I was a month in this voyage. We had one
violent storm but were able to stay on course.
On April 21, 1709, we cast anchor at the southeast
point of Luggnagg. We signaled to two boat pilots,
who rowed out to guide us in between the rocks.

Some of the sailors on my ship, whether out of treachery or error, informed the pilots that I was a stranger and a traveler, so the two pilots sent notice that a custom house[1] officer would need to examine me. This officer, who spoke Balnibarbi, asked for a short account of my travels, which I gave. I made my story as believable as I could. However, I thought it necessary to disguise my country and to say that I was Dutch, because I knew the Dutch were the only Europeans permitted to enter Japan. The officer said I must be imprisoned till he could receive orders from court. He would write immediately, and he hoped to receive an answer in about two weeks.

I passed several days in prison waiting for word from the court. The message came at the expected time. It contained an order for a party of ten horsemen to bring me to the capital. A messenger was sent half a day's journey ahead of us to give the King notice of my coming. He was to ask His Majesty to please appoint a day and hour when it would be his gracious pleasure that I might have the honor to lick the dust before his throne. This is the court style, and I found it to be

---

[1] custom house—government building or office where taxes on things brought into a country are collected.

more than a matter of form. When I was allowed into the throne room, two days after my arrival, I was commanded to crawl on my belly and lick the floor as I advanced. Because I was a stranger, care was taken to have it made so clean that the dust was not offensive. Of course, this was not always the case. I saw many instances, when the person had enemies at court, in which the floor was covered with dust on purpose, making the journey to the throne all the more unpleasant. At times, when the king has a mind to put any of his nobles to death in a gentle manner, he commands to have the floor covered with a certain poison, which being licked up, kills the person in twenty-four hours. There are strict orders that the floor be washed after one of these executions. If the servants don't do this, the King is displeased.

> *I was commanded to crawl on my belly and lick the floor as I advanced.*

To return from this **digression**,[2] when I had crept within four yards of the throne, I raised myself gently upon my knees and said many words of humble praise. The King was much

---

[2] **digression**—straying from the main subject.

delighted with my company. He ordered his servants to provide a lodging in the court for me and my interpreter, with a daily allowance for my food, and a large purse of gold for my expenses.

I stayed three months in this country out of perfect obedience to his Majesty. He asked me daily if I would stay on in his court for the rest of my years. But I thought it wiser and fairer to pass the remainder of my days with my wife and family.

Before I left, I was asked one day by a friend whether I had seen any Struldbrugs, or **immortal**[3] people. I asked for an explanation, and was told that sometimes a child was born with a red spot over the left eyebrow. This meant the child would never die. The spot changed color as the child grew older, from red to green to blue to black.

I said I would gladly pass my life here with such superior beings. I told them all the things I would do if I had the chance to be immortal. I would first do all that I could to become a rich man. In 200 years, I might be the richest man in the kingdom. Next, I would study the arts and sciences as thoroughly as I could. Lastly, I would carefully

---

[3] **immortal**—living forever.

write down the history of all the politics, customs, fashions, and languages so that I could become the wisest, most informed person in the world. Then I would educate others about the usefulness of good morals in public life.

My friend looked at me sadly. He explained that the Struldbrugs are nothing like I had imagined. They are immortal, true, but they age at the same rate as any man and are subject to the same illnesses and diseases that plague mortal men. They become sick at various times over the years, although they never die from their illnesses. Instead they must suffer the symptoms until some of them long for death.

Although he saw my look of horror, he continued with his description. After eighty years of life, he said, the Struldbrugs become forgetful and irritable, to the point that they can't remember their own names and the names of family members. They are looked on as dead by the law, their estates are inherited by their heirs, and they cannot be employed. At ninety, they lose their teeth and hair and can no longer feed themselves. They lose their ability to read because their eyesight is so poor and cannot talk because their throats are so weakened. Because they are such a burden, the Struldbrugs are hated by most people. When a child is born with the mark of a Struldbrug, it is cause for grief in the family. The reader will understand that my wish for immortality then greatly decreased.

My friend's description of the Struldbrugs convinced me even further that I had best make my way back home to England. I had no wish to meet such people, and I told my friend that I couldn't bear to hear anything else about them.

On May 6, 1709, I took a solemn leave of Luggnagg. A large boat carried me to Japan after a short fifteen days of travel. I spent a few weeks in a Japanese port town called Xamoschi, and then I was most pleased to board a ship bound for Europe. Nothing happened worth mentioning in this voyage.

On April 16, 1710, we put in at an English port. I left the boat the next morning and saw once more my native land after an absence of five years and six months. I went straight to Redriff, where I arrived the same day at two in the afternoon and found my wife and family in good health.

THE END OF THE THIRD PART

A Voyage to the
Houyhnhnms

I stayed at home with my wife and children for about five months in a very happy condition. I should have learned the lesson of knowing when I was well off. However, I soon found myself infected with the urge to travel. I left my poor wife big with child and accepted an advantageous offer to be captain of the *Adventure*, a stout ship of 350 tons. We set sail from Portsmouth on September 7, 1710.

I must say that trouble plagued my voyage right from the very start. Several men died of fevers, so I was forced to get fifty or so new sailors out of Barbados and the Leeward Islands. Later I regretted this move, as I found out that many of the new men I took on board were **buccaneers**.[1]

---

[1] **buccaneers**—pirates.

These **rogues**[2] convinced my other men to seize the ship and imprison me. One morning, they rushed into my cabin, tied me hand and foot, and threatened to throw me overboard if I moved. I told them I was their prisoner and would submit. This they made me swear to do, and then they unbound me. They fastened one of my legs with a chain near my bed

They rushed into my cabin, tied me hand and foot, and threatened to throw me overboard if I moved.

and placed at my door a guard who was commanded to shoot me dead if I attempted to escape. They sent me down food and drink and took over running the ship themselves. Their plan was to become pirates and **plunder**[3] the Spaniards, which they could not do until they got more men. But first they decided to sell the goods in the ship and then go to Madagascar for recruits. Several among them had died since my capture. They sailed many weeks and traded with the Indians. I did not know what way they went, as I was kept a prisoner in my cabin.

---

[2] **rogues**—rascals.
[3] **plunder**—rob.

On May 9, 1711, a seaman came down to my cabin and said he had orders from the Captain to set me ashore. I argued with him, but it made no difference. Several crew members forced me into a longboat. They rowed about three miles and then set me down on a small island. I asked them to tell me what country it was. They all swore they knew no more than I did. The Captain (as they called him) was determined to get rid of me in the first place where they could discover land. They pushed off immediately, advising me to hurry so that I would not be overtaken by the tide.

I sat down and considered what I should do. Finally, I decided to deliver myself to the first natives I should meet. I would buy my life from them with some bracelets, glass rings, and other toys I had about me. I walked carefully inland for fear of being surprised or shot at with an arrow from behind or on either side. I came to a road, where I saw many tracks of human feet, and some of cows, but most of horses. At last I saw several animals in a field and one or two of the same kind sitting in trees. Their shape was very ugly, which frightened me a little, so I lay down behind a **thicket**[4] to observe them better. Their heads and

---

[4] **thicket**—group of shrubs or underbrush.

chests were covered with a thick hair, some frizzled and others **lank**.[5] They had beards like goats and a long ridge of hair down their backs and on the foreparts of their legs and feet. The rest of their bodies was bare, so that I could see their skins, which were of a brown color. They had no tails nor any hair at all on their backs, except a little on their buttocks. They were able to climb high trees as nimbly as a squirrel, for they had strong, sharp claws. I saw them spring and bound and leap easily.

I also noticed that the females were not so large as the males. They had long lank hair on their heads, but none on their faces. The hair of both sexes was of several colors—brown, red, black, and yellow. Upon the whole, I never beheld in all my travels so ugly an animal, nor one for which I felt so much dislike. Thinking that I had seen enough, I got up and followed the road, hoping it might take me to the cabin of some native. I had not got far when I met one of these horrible-looking creatures in my path.

> *I had not got far when I met one of these horrible-looking creatures in my path.*

---

[5] **lank**—long, straight, and limp.

The ugly monster, when he saw me, stared as if he were seeing an object he had never seen before. Slowly, he approached nearer and lifted up his forepaw. Immediately, I drew my sword and gave him a good blow with the flat side of it. When the beast felt the smart, he drew back and roared so loud that a herd of at least forty came flocking about me from the next field, howling and making horrible faces. I ran to the trunk of a tree, leaned my back against it, and waved my sword in the air.

All of a sudden, however, the group of monsters turned toward the road and ran away as fast as they could. I wondered what had so frightened them. Looking around, I saw only a horse walking softly in the field. The horse started a little when he came near me but soon recovered himself, looked full in my face, and then walked around me several times. We stood gazing at each other for some time. At last I was bold enough to reach my hand towards his neck, with the idea of stroking it, in the same manner a jockey might use when he is going to handle a strange horse. But this animal seemed to receive my civilities with **disdain.**[6] He shook his head and bent his brows, softly raising up his right forefoot to remove my hand. Then he neighed three

---

[6] **disdain**—distaste.

or four times, but in such a way that I almost began to think he was speaking to himself in some language of his own.

Soon another horse came up and seemed to greet the first in a very gentle manner. The two horses gently struck each other's front right hoof and then neighed several times by turns. To my ears, their neighs and whinnies sounded almost **articulate.**[7] The two horses went some paces off, as if to talk together, walking side by side, backward and forward, like persons deliberating upon some important affair. I was amazed to see such actions and behavior in animals.

I decided to go forward until I could discover some house or village or meet with any of the natives, leaving the two horses to talk together as they pleased. But the first, who was a **dapple**[8] gray, observed me steal off. He neighed after me in so expressive a tone that I thought he meant that I should stay put.

The two horses came up close to me and examined me all over again. The gray horse stroked my right hand, seeming to admire the

---

[7] **articulate**—like a language.

[8] **dapple**—mottled or spotted marking, as on a horse's coat.

softness and color, but he squeezed it so hard between his hoof and his pastern[9] that I was forced to roar. After that they both touched me with all possible tenderness. Upon the whole, the behavior of these animals was so orderly and **rational**[10] that I at last concluded they must be magicians who had somehow changed themselves into horses. I decided to address them, and said the following:

> The behavior of these animals was so orderly and rational that I at last concluded they must be magicians.

"Gentlemen, if you be **conjurers**,[11] as I have good cause to believe you are, you can understand any language. Therefore I make bold to let your worships know that I am a poor distressed Englishman, driven by misfortunes upon your coast. I beg one of you to let me ride upon his back, as if he were a real horse, to some house or village. In return for this favor I will make you a present of this knife and bracelet."

---

[9] pastern—the part of a horse's foot between the fetlock (lower joint) and hoof.

[10] **rational**—sensible, reasonable.

[11] **conjurers**—magicians.

The two creatures stood silent while I spoke, seeming to listen with great attention. When I had finished, they neighed frequently towards each other, as if they were engaged in serious conversation. I could frequently distinguish the word *Yahoo*, which was repeated by each of them several times. Although it was impossible for me to understand what it meant, I tried to practice this word upon my tongue. As soon as they were silent, I boldly pronounced *Yahoo* in a loud voice, imitating, at the same time, as near as I could, the neighing of a horse. This surprised them greatly. The gray repeated the same word twice, as if he meant to teach me the right accent. I spoke after him as well as I could and found my pronunciation to improve every time. Then the **bay**[12] horse tried me with a second word, much harder to pronounce. This word was *Houyhnhnm*. I did not succeed so well with this word. After two or three additional trials, I had better luck, and they both appeared amazed at my ability.

After some further conversation, which I knew related to me, the two friends took their leave, with the same compliment of striking each other's hoof. The gray made me signs that I should walk before

---

[12] **bay**—a reddish-brown color.

him. When I would slow my pace, he would cry *Hhuun, Hhuun*. I guessed his meaning, and gave him to understand, as well as I could, that I was tired and not able to walk faster. Then he would stand a while to let me rest.

PART FOUR, CHAPTER TWO

Having traveled about three miles, we came to a long kind of building made of wood. The roof was low and covered with straw. The horse made me a sign to go in first, which I did. I saw that it was a large room with a smooth clay floor. It had a rack and **manger**[1] that extended the whole length on one side. There were three **nags**[2] and two **mares**,[3] not eating, but some of them sitting down upon their **hams**,[4] which I very much wondered at. I wondered even more to see the rest employed in household business. The gray came in just after me, and thereby prevented any ill treatment which the others might have given me. He neighed to them several times in a style of authority and received answers.

---

[1] **manger**—a trough or an open box in which feed for livestock is placed.

[2] **nags**—old or worn-out horses.

[3] **mares**—female horses.

[4] **hams**—buttocks.

Beyond this room there were three others. I walked into the second room and prepared my presents for the master and mistress of the house. I had two knives, three bracelets of false pearl, a small mirror, and a bead necklace. The horse neighed three or four times, and I waited to hear some answers in a human voice, but I heard none other than the same dialect, only one or two a little shriller than his. I began to think that this house must belong to some person of great importance, because there appeared so much ceremony before I could come in. Before I had time to truly look around, the gray horse came to the door and made me a sign to follow him into the third room. There I saw a very attractive mare, together with a **colt**[5] and **foal**[6] who were sitting on their **haunches**[7] upon mats of straw, which were perfectly neat and clean.

I began to think that this house must belong to some person of great importance.

The mare rose from her mat, and coming up close, after having closely observed my hands and face, gave me a most **contemptuous**[8] look. Turning

---

[5] **colt**—young male horse.

[6] **foal**—baby or infant horse.

[7] **haunches**—hips, buttocks, and upper thighs.

[8] **contemptuous**—scornful.

to the gray, she too said something about *Yahoo*. Later, when I understood the meaning of the word, I was humiliated. The gray, seeming to have reached a decision, again motioned for me to follow. We went to a new building, and here I saw three of those hateful creatures whom I first met after my landing. They were feeding upon roots and the flesh of some animals, which I afterwards found to be that of mules and dogs, and now and then they ate a cow dead by accident or disease. They were all tied by the neck with strong wires that were fastened to a beam. They held their food between the claws of their forefeet and tore it with their teeth.

The master horse ordered a **sorrel**[9] nag, one of his servants, to untie the largest of these animals and take him into the yard. The beast and I were brought close together and our appearances compared, both by master and servant, who thereupon repeated several times the word *Yahoo*. My horror and astonishment are not to be described when I

> **My horror and astonishment are not to be described when I observed in this awful animal a perfect human figure.**

---

[9] **sorrel**—brownish-orange to light brown.

observed in this awful animal a perfect human figure. The face of it indeed was flat and broad, the nose flat, the lips large, and the mouth wide. The forefeet of the Yahoo differed from my hands in nothing else but the length of the nails, the coarseness and brown color of the palms, and the hair on the backs. There was the same resemblance between our feet, with the same differences, which I knew very well, though the horses did not, because of my shoes and stockings.

The great difficulty that seemed to stick with the two horses was my clothing. They assumed that my body was different from the Yahoo's, but only because I was wearing clothes, which they had never seen before. The sorrel nag offered me a root. I took it in my hand and, having smelled it, returned it to him again as politely as I could. He brought out of the Yahoo's stall a piece of mule's flesh, but it smelled so bad that I turned from it with **loathing.**[10] He then threw it to the Yahoo, by whom it was greedily devoured. He afterwards showed me a wisp of hay and some oats, but I shook my head to show that neither of these were food for me.

In another moment, I noticed a cow passing by. I pointed to her and asked him to let me go

---

[10] **loathing**—disgust.

and milk her. This he understood. He led me back into the house and ordered a mare-servant to open a room where a good store of milk lay in earthen and wooden **vessels.**[11] She gave me a large bowl full. I drank very heartily and found myself well refreshed.

About noon I saw coming towards the house a kind of vehicle, drawn like a sled by four Yahoos. In it was an old **steed**[12] who seemed to be of quality. He got out with his back feet forward, having by accident got hurt in his left front foot. He came to dine with our horse, who received him with great civility. They dined in the best room and had oats boiled in milk for the second course, which the old horse ate warm, but the rest ate cold. The behavior of the young colt and foal appeared very modest, and that of the master and mistress extremely cheerful and welcoming to their guest. The gray ordered me to stand by him. Much conversation passed between him and his friend concerning me. Once again, I heard the word *Yahoo* repeated over and over again.

---

[11] **vessels**—containers.

[12] **steed**—horse.

When dinner was done, the master horse took me aside and by signs and words made me understand that he was concerned that I had nothing to eat. Oats in their tongue are called *hlunnh*. This word I pronounced two or three times. Although I had refused them at first, I had, in the meantime, decided I could use them to make a kind of bread that might be sufficient with milk to keep me alive. The horse immediately ordered a white mare-servant of his family to bring me a good quantity of oats in a sort of wooden tray. These I heated before the fire as well as I could and rubbed them till the husks came off. Then I ground the grain, added water, and made them into a small cake, which I ate warm with milk.

When it grew towards evening, the master horse ordered a place for me to lodge in. It was but six yards from the house and separated from the stable of the Yahoos. Here I got some straw, and covering myself with my own clothes, slept very well.

My main task for the next few weeks was to learn the language, which my master (for so I shall now call him) and his children, and every servant of his house, were anxious to teach me. I pointed to every thing and asked its name. These I wrote down in my journal when I was alone. I corrected my bad accent by asking those of the family to pronounce each word often.

The curiosity and impatience of my master were so great that he spent many hours instructing me. He was convinced (as he afterwards told me) that I must be a Yahoo, but my ability to learn, my politeness, and my cleanliness astonished him. These were not characteristic of Yahoos. He was most puzzled about my clothes, for I never pulled them off till the family was asleep and got them on before it awakened.

In about ten weeks' time, I was able to understand most of my master's questions, and in three months I could give him some brief answers. He was curious to know from what part of the country I came and how I was taught to imitate a rational creature. I answered that I came over the sea from a far place, with many others of my own kind, in a great hollow vessel made of the bodies of trees. It was with some difficulty, and by the help of many signs, that I brought him to understand me. He replied that I must be mistaken. He knew it was impossible that there could be a country beyond the sea, or that a group of brutes (as he thought of me) could move a wooden vessel wherever they pleased upon water. He was sure no Houyhnhnm alive could make such a vessel, nor would they trust Yahoos such as myself to manage it.

The word *Houyhnhnm* meant horse, and, in their meaning, *the perfection of nature*. Several high-born horses and mares who came to visit my master could not believe me to be a right Yahoo, because my body had a different covering from others of my kind. They were astonished to observe me without the usual hair or skin, except on my head, face, and hands. I have already told the reader that every night when the family had gone to bed, it was my habit to strip and cover myself with my clothes.

It happened one morning early that my master sent for me by the sorrel nag who was his **valet**.[1] When he came, I was fast asleep. My clothes had fallen off on one side, and my shirt was above my waist. I awakened at the noise he made, and heard him tell my master, in a great fright, that my body looked much different asleep than it did when I was awake. As soon as I was dressed, His Honor asked me the meaning of what his ser-

His Honor asked me the meaning of what his servant had reported, that I was not the same thing when I slept as I appeared to be at other times.

vant had reported, that I was not the same thing when I slept as I appeared to be at other times.

I had so far hidden the secret of my dress, in order to distinguish myself as much as possible from that cursed race of Yahoos. Now I found it impossible to do so any longer. I therefore told my master that in the country from which I came, those of my kind always covered their bodies with the hairs of certain animals prepared by art. These clothes, I said, were meant to protect us from the weather, in addition to maintaining some modesty. If he wished, I would show him what was under my clothes, but I

---

[1] **valet**—male servant.

told him I would prefer not to show those parts of my body nature had taught me to conceal.

He replied that my explanation was all very strange, especially the last part. He could not understand why nature should teach us to hide what nature had given. Neither he nor his family were ashamed of any parts of their bodies, he said, but he would allow me to do as I pleased. Upon hearing this, I unbuttoned my coat and pulled it off. I did the same with my waistcoat and then drew off my shoes, stockings, and breeches. I let my shirt down to my waist and drew up the bottom, fastening it like a **girdle**[2] about my middle to hide my nakedness.

My master observed the whole performance with great signs of curiosity and admiration. He took up all my clothes, one piece after another, and examined them carefully. Then he stroked my body very gently and looked round me several times. After this, he said it was plain I must be a perfect Yahoo. But I differed very much from the rest of my kind in the softness and whiteness and smoothness of my skin, my lack of hair in several parts of my body, the shape and shortness of my claws, and my habit of walking continually on my two back feet.

---

[2] **girdle**—belt or sash worn around the waist.

He desired to see no more and gave me permission to put on my clothes again, for I was shuddering with cold.

I expressed my uneasiness at his giving me so often the name of Yahoo, an **odious**[3] animal for which I had so utter a hatred and contempt. I begged he would resist applying that word to me and ask his family and friends to do the same. I likewise asked that he keep the secret of my clothes, so that no one would know except him and me and that he would command his valet not to tell what he had seen.

All this my master very graciously agreed to, and thus the secret was kept till my clothes began to wear out. In the meantime, he wanted me to go on with my work in learning their language. He was more astonished that I could speak and reason than at the figure of my body, whether it were covered or not. He added that he waited with some impatience to hear of the wonders that I promised to tell him.

Eventually, after much hard work, I was able to tell His Honor my story, which he listened to with great interest. I told him that I came from a very far

---

[3] **odious**—horrible.

country with about fifty others. We had traveled upon the seas in a great hollow boat made of wood. I described the ship to him in the best terms I could and explained, with the help of my handkerchief, how it was driven forward by the wind. I told of the quarrel on board, and how I came upon the horrible Yahoos. He asked me who made the ship and how it was possible that the Houyhnhnms of my country would leave it to the management of brutes? My answer was that I dare proceed no further in my story, unless he would give me his word of honor that he would not be offended. He agreed, and I went on. I told him that the ship was made by creatures such as myself. I told him that, in all the countries I had traveled to, as well as in my own, people like myself were the only governing, thinking animals. I said that, upon my arrival here, I was very surprised to see the Houyhnhnms act like rational beings. I said, furthermore, that if good fortune ever sent me back to my native country, everyone would believe that I had invented my story. My countrymen would think it was impossible that the Houyhnhnms were the masters and the Yahoos were the beasts.

PART FOUR, CHAPTER FOUR

My master listened to my stories with great uneasiness. When I said that the Yahoos were the masters in my country, he wanted to know whether we had Houyhnhnms among us and what were their jobs. I told him we had great numbers of Houyhnhnms. In the summer they grazed in the fields and in the winter were kept in houses with hay and oats. Yahoo servants were employed to rub their skins smooth, comb their manes, pick their feet, serve them with food, and make their beds. I said that the Houyhnhnms among us, whom we called horses, were the most attractive animals we had, and that they excelled in strength and swiftness. When they belonged to wealthy people, these horses were employed in traveling, racing, or drawing chariots and were treated with much kindness. But the common race of horses were not so lucky, since most were owned by people who put them to great labor and fed them very little. I described, as well as I could, how we rode horseback. I spoke of a horse's bridle, saddle, whip, harness,[1] and the wheels of a carriage. I added that we fastened plates of a certain hard substance called iron at the bottom of their feet to preserve their hoofs from being broken by the stony roads on which we often traveled.

My master, after telling me how disgusted he was, wondered how we dared to get up on a Houyhnhnm's back. He was sure that the weakest servant in his house would be able to shake off the strongest Yahoo. I answered that our horses were trained from three or four years old to allow a rider to saddle them. If any of them could not be ridden, they were used to pull carriages. I also said that while they were young, horses were severely beaten for any mischievous tricks and that the males were generally **castrated**[2] about two years after their birth, to make them tamer.

It was difficult to tell my master this story. The Houyhnhnm language is a simple one because their wants and passions are fewer than ours. It

---

[1] bridle, saddle, whip, harness—equipment put on a horse when it is ridden or used to pull a wagon or carriage.

[2] **castrated**—made unable to reproduce by having the testicles removed.

was also difficult because he was so outraged by what I told him. Yahoos were not fit to run a country, he exclaimed. Furthermore, he continued angrily, all animals on Earth instinctively hate the filthy Yahoo.

After he had calmed himself, he said that he would debate the matter no further because he was still so interested to hear about my life. I assured him I would do my best to explain. I told my personal history and then went on to give the history of England. Some of its history was easy for my master to understand. Some of it, however, was nearly impossible because the Houyhnhnms have no words for such things as *power, government, war, law,* and *punishment.*

Over the next two years, I had many, many conversations with my master. I laid before him, as well as I could, the whole state of Europe. I discussed trade and manufacturing, arts and sciences, and politics and government.

At one point, during my description of war, His Honor commanded me to stop talking because he was so sickened by what I was saying. Although he hated the Yahoos of this country (he explained), he no more blamed them for their horrible qualities than he did a bird of prey for its cruelty. But the Yahoos of this Europe—they were to blame for their ugliness. They pretended to be rational creatures, yet they went to war with one another, killing without reason and justification. They were brutal and horrible, and far, far worse than the

Yahoos that he and his fellow Houyhnhnms had to deal with.

My master was wholly unable to understand why my fellow Yahoos acted the way they did. He couldn't understand the treachery, dishonesty, and murderous habits of the Europeans, and at times I was truly at a loss to explain.

The reader may wonder how I could bring myself to talk so openly about my own kind to one who clearly had the vilest opinion of humans. It is true that His Honor was disgusted by us, but I must admit that I had begun to share his disgust. The Houyhnhnms are a virtuous, peaceful race, I discovered. By comparison, human beings are filled with faults and **infirmities**.[1] Furthermore, I had learned from my master to hate all falsehoods and disguises. It would have been impossible for me to tell any story unless it was the strictest truth. Let me also say that I had not been a year in this country before I developed such a love and **veneration**[2] for the inhabitants that I made a firm promise to myself never to return to humankind but to pass the rest of my life among these admirable Houyhnhnms.

---

[1] **infirmities**—ailments or weaknesses.
[2] **veneration**—feeling of awe and respect.

When at last I had answered all His Honor's questions and his curiosity seemed to be fully satisfied, he sent for me one morning early and commanded me to sit down. He said he had been very seriously considering my whole story and had drawn some conclusions, which I will state here. He told me that it was obvious that I had neither the strength or agility of a common Yahoo. I walked with some difficulty on my back feet. I had found a way to make my claws useless for self-defense, and I could neither run with speed, nor climb trees like the Yahoos in this country.

He also believed that our institutions of government and law were plainly a result of our gross defects in reason.

He also believed that our institutions of government and law were plainly a result of our **gross**[3] defects in reason and, consequently, in virtue. He observed that Yahoos were known to hate one another more than they did any different kind of animal. The reason was usually believed to be on account of their ugliness, which all could see in others, but not in themselves. He had therefore begun to think it wise of us to cover our bodies,

---

[3] **gross**—extreme.

thereby hiding our **deformities**[4] from each other. He finished by explaining his theory that if you throw among five Yahoos as much food as would be enough for fifty, they will, instead of eating peaceably, fight for as much as each can get. Each single one is impatient to have all to itself.

He also told me that in some fields of his country there are certain shiny stones of several colors. The Yahoos are violently fond of them, and when parts of these stones are fixed in the earth, as it sometimes happens, they will dig with their claws for whole days to get them out. Then they carry them away and hide them by heaps in their stalls. They use great caution for fear their comrades should discover their treasure. My master said he could never discover the reason of this unnatural appetite for stones, or how these stones could be of any use to a Yahoo. Now he believed it might come from the same principle of greed which I had connected to humankind. My master further assured me that the fiercest and most frequent battles are fought in the fields where the most shining stones are found. All this because the Yahoos so desire these stones.

---

[4] **deformities**—improperly made body parts.

Because I wanted to better understand the Yahoos and find out if my master was right that human beings truly are of the Yahoo breed, I asked permission to go among the herds of Yahoos in the neighborhood. He agreed and asked one of his servants, a strong sorrel nag, to be my guard. Without this protection I dared not undertake such adventures, for I have already told the reader how much I was pestered by those horrible animals upon my arrival.

I learned that these Yahoos are nimble from their infancy. However, I once caught a young male of three years old and tried to make it quiet. The little imp fell a-squalling and scratching and biting with such violence that I was forced to let it go. It was high time, for a whole troop of old ones came around us at the noise. Finding the cub was safe (for away it ran) and my sorrel nag being by, they dared not come near us. I observed the young animal's flesh to smell very foul—somewhat between a weasel and a fox, but much more disagreeable.

I also discovered that the Yahoos are the most unteachable of all animals.

I also discovered that the Yahoos are the most unteachable of all animals. I believe this defect arises chiefly from a difficult, restless personality, for they are cunning, malicious, and treacherous. They are strong and hardy but of a cowardly spirit and, as a result, they are **insolent**[1] and cruel.

The Houyhnhnms keep some Yahoos as servants. The rest are sent abroad to certain fields, where they dig up roots, eat several kinds of herbs, and search about for game. They swim from their infancy like frogs, and they are able to stay underwater a long time. They often catch fish, which the females carry home to their young. And, at this point, I hope the reader will pardon my relating an odd adventure.

---

[1] **insolent**—offensively rude; arrogant.

Being one day abroad with the sorrel nag, and the weather being exceedingly hot, I begged him to let me bathe in a river that was near. He agreed, and I immediately stripped myself stark naked and went down into the stream. It happened that a young female Yahoo, standing behind a bank, saw me and became inflamed by desire (as the nag and I later guessed). She came running with all speed and leaped into the water within five yards of the place where I bathed. I was never in my life so terribly frightened. The Yahoo embraced me. I roared as loud as I could, and the nag came galloping towards me. Only then did the Yahoo let go. She leaped upon the opposite bank and stood gazing and howling all the time I was putting on my clothes.

I could no longer deny that I was a real Yahoo, since the females had a natural attraction to me.

This was a matter of entertainment to my master and his family, as well as of embarrassment to myself. For now I could no longer deny that I was a real Yahoo, since the females had a natural attraction to me as one of their own kind.

Because I lived three years in this country, the reader will expect that I should, like other travelers, tell about the manners and customs of its people. The great principle of the Houyhnhnms is to cultivate reason and to be wholly governed by it. Friendship and kindness are their two main virtues. A stranger from the remotest part of the world is treated just like the nearest neighbor. Wherever he goes abroad, he looks upon himself as at home. They preserve decency and civility in the highest degrees but are altogether ignorant of ceremony. They have no fondness for their colts or foals. The care they take in educating them proceeds entirely from reason. And I observed my master to show the same affection to his neighbor's offspring that he had for his own. Nature has taught them to love the whole species, and the only difference between them is their ability to reason.

In their marriages they are careful to choose such colors as will not make any disagreeable mixture in the breed. Strength is chiefly valued in the male, and attractiveness in the female. They do not choose mates on account of love, but to preserve the race. When a female happens to excel in strength, then a **consort**[1] is chosen with regard to attractiveness. Courtship, love, and gifts have no place in their thoughts. The young couple meet and are joined merely because their parents and friends have decided on it. This is what they see done every day, and they look upon it as one of the necessary actions of a rational being. But unfaithfulness in marriage, or any other unchastity,[2] is unheard of. The married pair pass their lives with the same friendship and mutual kindness that they bear to all others of the same species who come their way, without jealousy, fondness, or quarreling.

In raising their young, their methods are admirable and highly deserving of our imitation. They are not allowed to taste a grain of oats, except upon certain days, till they are eighteen years old.

---

[1] **consort**—mate; husband.

[2] unchastity—unfaithfulness; adultery.

In summer, they graze two hours in the morning and two hours in the evening, which their parents also do. Servants are not allowed more than half that time, and a great part of their grass is brought home for them to eat only when they can be spared from work. **Temperance,**[3] industry, exercise, and cleanliness are the lessons taught to young ones of both sexes. My master thought it monstrous in us to give the females a different kind of education from the males. The Houyhnhnms train their youth for strength, speed, and hardiness.

Every fourth year, at the vernal equinox,[4] there is a representative Council of the whole nation. It meets in a plain about twenty miles from our house, and continues about five or six days. Here they inquire into the state and condition of the several districts, such as whether they have enough hay, oats, cows, or Yahoos. Wherever there is any want (which is seldom), it is immediately supplied by unanimous consent and contribution. Here, likewise, the regulation of children is settled. For instance, if a Houyhnhnm has two males, he exchanges one of them with another that has two females. When a child has died, it is decided what family in the district shall breed another to supply the loss.

---

[3] **Temperance**—moderation.

[4] vernal equinox—time in the spring when day and night are of equal length.

One of these representative Councils was held in my time, about three months before my departure. My master went as the representative of our district. This Council continued the old debate, and indeed, the only debate that ever happened in that country. My master, after his return, gave me a very detailed account.

The question debated was whether the Yahoos should be destroyed from the face of the Earth. One of the members in favor of it offered several arguments of great strength and weight, **alleging**[5] that the Yahoos were the most filthy, **noisome,**[6] and deformed animals that nature ever produced. Yahoos, he said, had not always been in that country. Many ages ago, two of these brutes appeared together upon a mountain. Maybe they were produced by the heat of the sun upon corrupted mud and slime, or from the ooze and froth of the sea. Their true origin was never known. The Houyhnhnms tried to get rid of this evil, but did not succeed.

Several others declared their similar beliefs. Then my master proposed a solution, whereof he had indeed borrowed the hint from me. He said that he had in his possession a wonderful Yahoo

5 **alleging**—asserting.
6 **noisome**—foul.

184 **Gulliver's Travels**

(meaning myself), which most of them had heard of and many of them had seen. He then explained to them how he first found me. He told them I spoke in a language of my own and had thoroughly learned theirs. I looked exactly like a Yahoo, except I was of a whiter color, less hairy, and with shorter claws. He added that he observed in me all the qualities of a Yahoo, only I was a little more civilized.

He continued thus: his Yahoo (myself) had mentioned a custom we had of castrating Houyhnhnms when they were young, in order to render them tame. The operation was easy and safe. This invention, he said, might be practiced upon the younger Yahoos here. Besides making them obedient and more fit for use, this practice would eventually destroy the whole species without destroying life. In the meantime, the Houyhnhnms should be **exhorted**[7] to cultivate the breed of mules, which, as they are in all respects more valuable brutes, might replace the Yahoos as servants.

He observed in me all the qualities of a Yahoo, only I was a little more civilized.

---

[7] **exhorted**—urged by strong argument.

This was all my master thought fit to tell me at that time of what passed in the grand Council. But he was pleased to hide one thing that related personally to myself. I learned of this unhappy detail later, as the reader will soon know.

The Houyhnhnms have no alphabet, and consequently their knowledge is all passed on by word of mouth. They calculate the year by the revolution of the sun and the moon but use no subdivisions into weeks. Their stories and poetry are exceedingly beautiful, as they have such keen ears for description.

Their buildings, although very simple, are designed to defend them from all injuries of cold and heat. The Houyhnhnms use the hollow part between their pasterns and forefeet as we do our hands, and better than I could at first imagine. I have seen a white mare of our family thread a needle (which I lent her on purpose) with that joint. They milk their cows, reap their oats, and do all the work that requires hands in the same manner. They have a kind of hard stone flint, which, by grinding against other stones, they form into instruments that serve as wedges, axes, and hammers. With tools made of these flints, they likewise cut their hay and reap their oats.

I f they can avoid accidents, they die only of old age and are buried in the most obscure places that can be found. Their friends and relations express neither joy nor grief at their departure, nor does the dying person feel the least regret that he is leaving the world.

They live generally to seventy or seventy-five years, but very seldom to eighty. Some weeks before their death, they feel a gradual decay, but without pain. During this time, they are often visited by their friends, because they cannot go abroad with their usual ease and satisfaction. However, about ten days before their death, which they seldom fail in computing, they return the visits that have been made them by those who are nearest in the neighborhood. For these visits, they are carried about in a sled drawn by Yahoos. Therefore, when the dying Houyhnhnms return those visits, they take a solemn leave of their friends, as if they were going to some remote part of the country to pass the rest of their lives.

I could enlarge further upon the manners and virtues of these excellent people; but intend soon to publish a book on that subject. I refer the reader, therefore to that book and, in the meantime, proceed to tell my own sad story.

It is impossible to describe how comfortable I had become on the island of the Houyhnhnms. I had a comfortable room and an excellent mattress made from straw. I had made two chairs with my knife. The sorrel nag helped me with the more difficult parts. When my clothes were worn to rags, I made myself others with the skins of rabbits and another small animal of the same size whose skin is covered with a fine down. Of these I made very good stockings. I soled my shoes with wood I cut from a tree and fitted to the upper leather, and when this was worn out, I used the skins of Yahoos dried in the sun. I often got honey out of hollow trees, which I mixed with water or ate with my bread. No man could be more sure of the truth of these two **maxims**,[1] *That nature is very easily satisfied*; and *That necessity is the mother of invention.* I enjoyed perfect health of body and peace of mind. I did not feel the treachery or **inconstancy**[2] of a

---

[1] **maxims**—general truths or rules of conduct.

[2] **inconstancy**—fickleness; changing from friendly to distant.

friend nor the injuries of a secret or open enemy. Here was neither doctor to destroy my body nor lawyer to ruin my fortune. No pickpockets, dungeons, axes. No cheating shopkeepers or mechanics. No pride or vanity. No drunks or bullies. No loud or expensive wives. No lords, judges, or dancing masters.

My friends often tell me in a blunt way that I trot like a horse.

When I thought of my family, friends, or the human race in general, I considered them as they really were: Yahoos. Perhaps they were a little more civilized and improved by the gift of speech, but they were totally unreasonable and unhappy. When I happened to see my own reflection in a lake or fountain, I turned away my face in horror and hatred of myself. I could better stand the sight of a common Yahoo than of my own person. By talking with the Houyhnhnms and looking upon them with delight, I started to imitate their **gait**[3] and gesture, which is now grown into a habit. My friends often tell me in a blunt way that I trot like a horse. When I speak, I am apt to fall into the voice and manner

---

[3] **gait**—way of moving.

of the Houyhnhnms. I hear myself ridiculed on that account without the least embarrassment.

In the midst of all this happiness, and when I looked upon myself to be fully settled for life, my master sent for me one morning a little earlier than his usual hour. I noticed that he was slow to say what he had to say. After a short silence, he told me what was said in the last Council. When the Yahoos were discussed, the representatives had taken offense at his keeping a Yahoo (meaning myself) in his family and treating him more as a Houyhnhnm than a brute animal. He was known frequently to talk with me, as if he could receive some advantage or pleasure in my company. Such a practice was not agreeable to reason or nature. Such a thing was never heard of before among them. The Council therefore insisted that he would have to either use me like the rest of my kind or order me to swim back to the place from where I came. The assembly feared that, because I had some ability to reason, I might be able to convince my fellow Yahoos to revolt and destroy the Houyhnhnm community.

Because he knew me so well, my master was aware that the first option was not really an option at all—I could never be used like the rest of the Yahoos. However, he also knew that it would be impossible for me to swim to another country. Therefore, he had decided to ask me to build some sort of boat like those I had described to him to carry me on the sea. He would have his own servants help me so that I might finish the job in a timely manner.

I was struck with the utmost grief and despair at my master's words, and I fell into a **swoon**[4] at his feet. When I came to myself, he told me that he had concluded that I was dead (for these people are never subject to fainting spells). I answered in a faint voice that death would have been too great a happiness. Although I could not blame the Council's decision, I was deeply saddened by it. I explained that I knew that I could not swim the distance to the nearest land, as it was above three hundred miles away. I also knew that it would be impossible to build a seaworthy vessel, as I lacked so many of the necessary materials. I would, however, submit to my master's orders, although I secretly preferred the prospect of death. I could not bear the thought of returning to life among the human Yahoos.

---

[4] **swoon**—faint.

My master made me a very gracious reply and allowed me two months to finish my boat. He then ordered the sorrel nag, my fellow servant, to help me.

In the company of this nag, my first business was to go to that part of the coast where my rebellious crew had ordered me to be set on shore. I climbed on a rock and looked out upon the sea. I fancied I saw a small island towards the northeast. I took out my pocket glass and could then clearly see it about fifteen miles off. After I had discovered this island, I resolved it should, if possible, be the first place of my exile.

I returned home and then went into the woods where I cut down several oak branches about the thickness of a walking stick and some larger pieces. I shall not trouble the reader with a particular description of all my work. Let me say, though, that in six weeks' time, with the help of the sorrel nag, I finished a sort of Indian canoe, but much larger. It was covered with the skins of Yahoos well stitched together with woven threads of my own making. My sail was likewise made from the skins of the same animal. But I made use of the youngest I could get, the older being too tough and thick. I provided myself with four paddles, laid in some boiled rabbits and fowls, and took with me two jars, one filled with milk and the other with water.

I tried my canoe in a large pond near my master's house, and then corrected what was not right. I filled all the holes with Yahoos' tallow,[5] until I found it seaworthy and able to bear me and my belongings. And when it was as complete as I could possibly make it, I had it drawn on a carriage very gently by Yahoos to the seaside.

> **I said goodbye to my master and lady and the whole family. My eyes were flowing with tears, and my heart quite sunk with grief.**

When all was ready and the day came for me to leave, I said goodbye to my master and lady and the whole family. My eyes were flowing with tears, and my heart quite sunk with grief. But His Honor, out of curiosity, and perhaps (if I may speak it without vanity) partly out of kindness, was determined to see me in my canoe. He got several of his neighboring friends to accompany him. I was forced to wait over an hour for the tide. When I saw the wind very fortunately blowing towards the island to which I intended to steer my course, I took a second leave of my master. As

---

[5] tallow—hard fat.

I was going to my knees to kiss his hoof, he did me the honor to raise it gently to my mouth. I paid my respects to the rest of the Houyhnhnms in His Honor's company. Then I got into my canoe and pushed off from shore.

I began this desperate voyage on February 15, 1714, at 9 o'clock in the morning. The wind was very favorable, allowing me to sail at a rate of a league and a half an hour. My master and his friends stayed on the shore till I was almost out of sight, and I often heard the sorrel nag (who always loved me) crying out, *"Hnuy illa nyha majah Yahoo,"* which translates to "Take care of yourself, gentle Yahoo."

My plan was, if possible, to discover some small uninhabited island where I could spend the rest of my days. The idea of returning to live in the society and under the government of Yahoos was so horrible. I would spend my days alone, able to enjoy my thoughts and reflect with delight on the virtues of those **inimitable**[1] Houyhnhnms.

---

[1] **inimitable**—matchless.

Although I wasn't sure where in the vast world I was, I did believe that my mutinous crew had set me down about ten degrees south of the Cape of Good Hope.[2] Therefore, I decided to steer my course eastward, hoping to reach the southwest coast of New Holland and perhaps some deserted island close by.

The wind was full west, and by six in the evening I computed I had gone eastward at least fifty-four miles. Then I saw a very small island about a mile and a half off, which I soon reached. It was nothing but a rock, with one creek, naturally arched by the force of storms. Here I put in my canoe and climbed up a part of the rock. I could plainly discover land to the east, extending from south to north. I lay all night in my canoe and then repeated my voyage early in the morning. In seven hours, I arrived at the southeast point of New Holland.

I saw no people in the place where I landed. Being unarmed, I was afraid of going too far into the country. I found some shellfish on the shore and ate them raw, not daring to kindle a fire for fear of being discovered by the natives. For three days, I fed on oysters and limpets[3] to save my own

---

[2] Cape of Good Hope—near the southern tip of Africa.

[3] limpets—small marine mollusks.

food. I fortunately found a brook of excellent water, which gave me great relief.

On the fourth day, going out early a little too far, I saw twenty or thirty natives not more than five hundred yards from me. They were stark naked, men, women, and children, round a fire. One of them saw me and gave notice to the rest. Five of them advanced towards me, leaving the women and children at the fire. I hurried to the shore and, getting into my canoe, shoved off. When they saw me leaving, the natives ran after me. Before I could get far enough into the sea, one discharged an arrow that wounded me deeply on the inside of my left knee. (I shall carry the mark to my grave.) I feared the arrow might be poisoned, so I sucked at the wound and bandaged it as well as I could.

I didn't know what to do, for I dared not return to the same landing place. I paddled to the north, and soon saw a sail on the horizon. I was in some doubt whether I should sail toward it or not. At last my hatred of the Yahoo race took over and, turning my canoe, I sailed and paddled to the south. I got into the same creek from which I set out in the morning, choosing rather to trust myself among these natives than to live with European Yahoos. I drew up my canoe as close as I could to the shore, and hid myself behind a stone by the little brook.

The ship came within a mile and a half of this creek and sent her longboat out with vessels to take in fresh water. I did not notice it, however, until the boat was almost on shore and it was too late to seek another hiding place. The seamen saw my canoe and guessed that the owner could not be far off. Four well-armed men searched every cranny and hiding-hole. At last they found me flat on my face behind the stone. They looked for a while in surprise at my strange **uncouth**[4] dress, my coat made of skins, my wooden-soled shoes, and my furred stockings. They must have concluded, however, that I was not a native of the place, since the natives go naked.

One of the seamen told me in Portuguese to rise and asked who I was. I understood that language very well and, getting upon my feet, said I was a poor Yahoo banished from the Houyhnhnms. I asked them to please leave me alone. They were surprised to hear me answer them in their own tongue. They saw by my skin I must be a European but didn't know what I meant by Yahoos and

---

[4] **uncouth**—crude.

Houyhnhnms. At the same time, they laughed at my strange tone in speaking, which resembled the neighing of a horse. I trembled all the while between fear and hatred. Again I asked permission to depart and was slowly moving toward my canoe when they grabbed me and asked what country I was from.

I told them I was born in England, from which I came about five years ago, and at that time their country and ours were at peace. I therefore hoped they would not treat me as an enemy, since I meant them no harm. But, being a poor Yahoo, I was only seeking some lonely place to pass the remainder of my unfortunate life.

They spoke to me with humanity and said they were sure the Captain would carry me **gratis**[5] to Lisbon, Spain. From there, I might return to my own country. They told me that two of the seamen would go back to the ship, tell the Captain what they had seen, and receive instructions.

In two hours, their longboat returned with the Captain's command to take me aboard. I fell on my knees and begged for my freedom, but it was in vain. The men tied me with cords and heaved

---

[5] **gratis**—free.

me into the boat. I was taken immediately to the Captain's cabin.

The Captain's name was Pedro de Mendez. He was a very courteous and generous person. He begged me to give some account of myself and asked what I would eat or drink. He said so many courteous and helpful things that I was amazed to find such politeness from a Yahoo. However, I remained silent and sullen. I was ready to faint at the very smell of him and his men. At last I asked for something to eat out of my own canoe, but

After dinner, Don Pedro came to me and desired to know why I tried to escape.

he ordered me a chicken and some excellent wine. He then directed that I should be put to bed in a very clean cabin. I would not undress myself. I lay on the bed-clothes and, in half an hour, stole out when I thought the crew was at dinner. I attempted to jump into the sea and swim for my life rather than continue among the Yahoos, but one of the seamen prevented me. He informed the Captain, who chained me to my cabin.

After dinner, Don Pedro came to me and desired to know why I tried to escape, assuring me that he only meant to help me. He spoke so very movingly that at last I decided to treat him like an animal that had some little portion of reason. I gave him a very short explanation of my voyage, of the conspiracy against me by my own men, and of the country where they set me on shore. The Captain, a wise man, believed my story. During the course of our voyage, I told him more of my adventures and for the most part managed to conceal my **revulsion**[6] of him.

We arrived at Lisbon on November 5, 1715. At our landing, the Captain forced me to cover myself with his cloak to prevent the people from crowding about me. I was taken to his own house, and at my earnest request he led me to a solitary room. The Captain persuaded me to accept a suit of clothes newly made, which I aired for twenty-four hours before I would use them.

After many days, I came to tolerate the Captain's company. By degrees I was brought into another room. In a week's time I found my terror gradually lessened, but my hatred and contempt seemed to increase. At last, I was brave enough to leave his house on short trips, although I found the presence

---

[6] **revulsion**—deep-rooted dislike; disgust.

of so many Yahoos very disturbing. It helped to keep my nose well-stopped with lavender or tobacco. Don Pedro believed that I ought to return to my native country and live at home with my wife and children. He told me there was an English ship in the port just ready to sail, and he would give me everything I would need for the journey.

It would be **tedious**[7] to repeat his arguments and my contradictions. He said it was altogether impossible to find such a deserted island as I had desired to live in. I could find **solitude**[8] in my own house and pass my time as I pleased.

I agreed at last, finding I could not do better. I left Lisbon on November 24, in an English merchant ship. Don Pedro went with me to the ship and lent me twenty pounds. He took kind leave of me and embraced me at parting, which I bore as well as I could. During this last voyage, I had no interaction with the master or any of his men. Pretending I was sick, I kept to my cabin. On December 5, 1715, we cast anchor in an English port about nine in the morning, and at three in the afternoon I got safe to my house at Redriff.

My wife and family received me with great surprise and joy, because they thought I was long dead. But I must freely confess the sight of them

---

[7] **tedious**—tiresome.
[8] **solitude**—condition of being alone.

filled me only with hatred, disgust, and contempt. As soon as I entered the house, my wife took me in her arms and kissed me. As I had not been used to the touch of humans for so many years, I fell into a faint for almost an hour.

I am writing this five years after my last return to England. During the first year, I could not stand having my wife or children near me. The very smell of them was intolerable. To this hour, they dare not touch my bread or drink out of the same cup, and I am completely unable to let one of them take me by the hand. The first money I laid out was to buy two young horses, which I keep in a good stable. My horses understand me fairly well. I talk with them at least four hours every day. They are strangers to bridle or saddle and live in great friendship with me and each other.

Thus, gentle reader, I have given you a faithful history of my travels for sixteen years and seven months. I have told only the truth in these tales, for my main aim was to inform, and not to amuse. Having said this, I here take a final leave of all my courteous readers and return to enjoy my own little garden at Redriff. I hope to apply those excellent lessons of virtue that I learned among the Houyhnhnms and to teach the Yahoos of my own family as much as I can.

I began last week to permit my wife to sit at dinner with me, at the farthest end of a long table. And although it is hard for a man late in life to remove old habits, I do believe that some day I might be able to stand the company of a neighboring Yahoo or two, as long as they are no threat to my safety.

Even so, each time I behold an ugly lump or disease, either in mind or body, or evidence of vice or wickedness in my fellow Yahoos, I feel an unspeakable revulsion. This, I believe, will continue for the rest of my life. Therefore, I beg those who have any type of ugliness or vice within them not to come in my sight.

THE END